PERSONAL COUNSELLING

PERSONAL
COUNSELLING

An Introduction to
Relationship Therapy

J. H. WALLIS

with a Foreword by
Sir George Haynes
C.B.E.

London
GEORGE ALLEN & UNWIN LTD
Ruskin House   Museum Street

ISBN 0 04 361015 3 Hardback
0 04 361016 1 Paperback

Printed in Great Britain
in 10 point Baskerville type
by Clarke, Doble & Brendon Ltd
Plymouth

FOREWORD

by Sir George Haynes G.B.E.

President of the Standing Conference for the Advancement of Counselling

I welcome the invitation to write a foreword to this book because I believe it makes a most valuable and timely contribution to the study and practice of counselling. During the past few years a remarkable increase has taken place in the number and variety of agencies providing some form of counselling service. Many are new and have been created to meet some pressing need for aid for particular groups of people – for the young, in education and employment; for those suffering from a mental or physical handicap; for adults undergoing acute stress at home, at work or in the community; for older people who succumb to the pressures of our complex and, to them, bewildering society. Some of the agencies are long-established bodies which are seeking fresh ways of providing their personal services, more in tune with contemporary situations. Established professions would seem to be more aware that their skilled specialist services need to be more sensitively attuned to basic human needs and to the unique personal situations which sometimes confront their clients.

I am convinced that this growth of counselling activities is not a passing phase of social and professional organization but is the result of a new awareness of critical human problems produced or aggravated by the dynamic forces which are shaping our society. This belief is powerfully reinforced by the range and diversity of interest expressed in the recently established Standing Conference for the Advancement of Counselling, which has been established to provide a national focus for agencies concerned to meet some of the urgent needs of the individual. Its membership includes professional associations in education, medicine and the law, religious denominations and their pastoral care units, welfare societies for the handicapped, associations for educational and vocational guidance, associations of teachers, youth leaders and students, advisory bodies for immigrants and other groups, university training departments and research organizations. All these agencies have an active interest in counselling services and have joined together in the establishment of the Conference to deepen their knowledge of counselling in its different forms and to promote co-operation between them. For some of these agencies counselling is a primary purpose, for others it is a supporting element in a service with wider purposes. In some cases it is conducted entirely by professionals, in others by trained voluntary workers, and of course in widely differing settings. In spite of this diversity of operation there is a growing consensus of view about the nature of counselling conceived as a constructive and disciplined contribution to human needs. It should be a relationship in which the one counselled is enabled to see his personal problems more clearly and objectively and make his choices with reduced anxiety and tension. It is a two-way form of communication – a caring relationship which may well make searching demands on the counsellor, and requires adequate training and continuous preparation whether he be professional or layman.

At the inaugural meeting of the Conference Dr J. D. Sutherland, former Director of the Tavistock Clinic, defined counselling as 'a personal relationship in which the counsellor uses his own experience of himself to help his client to enlarge his understanding and so to make better decisions. The process of counselling is an educational activity for both parties and each encounter is unique.'

All counsellors will share a basic interest in this form of educational activity, and I believe will find in this book much that will extend and reinforce their understanding of their roles. Mr Wallis is richly endowed to write on Personal Counselling. His experience covers an exceptional range of activities as teacher, counsellor, trainer of counsellors, writer and lecturer in this country and overseas. He was the first full-time training officer of the National Marriage Guidance Council and has directed training courses abroad. His contacts with many kinds of groups concerned with counselling enables him to write with a close knowledge of the attitudes and problems of those who practise it. I have found his book most sensitively written and containing many insights into human responses, deepened, I feel sure, by his own direct experiences of helping people in difficulties. I am confident that it contains much of practical interest to all kinds of counsellors – to members of the psychotherapuetic professions, to counsellors within religious, educational and welfare organizations, and to all who wish to equip themselves to play some constructive part in this growing service.

George Haynes

CONTENTS

AUTHOR'S NOTE

This book is written for anyone who works with individuals in a helping capacity, or is training to do so. It aims to provide him with a bridge between the personal and the impersonal, specialized or technical aspects of his job.

Those clients or patients who are emotionally distressed or in some state of psychological conflict are usually unable to accept expert advice. Still less can they act on it. They may be unable to make a decision, however necessary. And sometimes they are unable to avoid creating or increasing their own problems compulsively and against their own interests. Their resulting distress may be intense and it is not easy to help them.

Such people present a particular kind of challenge. Their immediate need is not so much for expert information or specialized advice or direction as for skilled help of a personal kind. The problem they present is inaccessible to reason or even to common-sense. Indeed, they often know what they should do but are unable to do it. This common predicament and human need gives rise to the ever-increasing demand for personal counselling. This need arises at any time in any profession or vocation in which there is a personal relationship between the two parties, helper and client.

The present book arises directly from the author's experience, over the past eleven years, of working with small in-service training groups that meet regularly (usually once a week) over periods of between six weeks and three years. Some of these groups have comprised people from one particular discipline. Sometimes they have been composed of members of various professions and vocations and occasionally of various nationalities also. The common ground between the members has been the need for personal counselling in those who have come for help.

These groups have included child care officers, health visitors, youth workers, student-counsellors, doctors, prison officers, welfare officers, clergy, solicitors, social workers in many different settings, nurses, teachers, medical auxiliaries, and marriage counsellors. All were qualified in their own field, yet they were colleagues and equals in the personal aspects of their work. Many of them were already trained in casework and familiar with its literature. But when it comes to free discussion of problems and conflicts presented in daily experience, every situation is new and unique. And in this sense everyone is a beginner, no matter how experienced.

The present book therefore concentrates on the worker (the counsellor) rather than on the hypothetical client or patient. I am convinced that this is the area which determines the degree of help that can be given to individuals in distress or difficulty. Counselling is not a technique that can be wholly learnt from a book or from lectures. It is a practical way of helping people. It depends on the ability and personality of the helper as much as on the terms in which the problem is presented to him. Therefore, in my view, the accepted textbooks on casework and counselling (excellent as most of them are) need to be supplemented by a consideration not of theory but of the impact that such work makes on the individual reader-counsellor.

Sometimes the didactic quality of casework literature seems to me to fail in practising what it preaches. Some authorities in effect advise counsellors never to advise their clients. Some demand almost superhuman qualities in the caseworker while telling him never to make demands of his clients. Such contradictions can scarcely be avoided if one follows a conventional textbook or academic approach. I have therefore used a different approach in these pages. This is to examine the key issues in personal work of this kind from different angles so that the reader can get a wider view of them on which to base his own assessment.

Such key issues include the quality of the relationships between counsellor and client, the kind of change aimed at, the significance of unconscious factors and what the counsellor can do about them, the values implicit in any counselling or casework role, the boundaries of counselling, casework and psychotherapy, and the tricky question of personal involvement. It is no part of my purpose to indicate what anyone acting as a counsellor should think about these issues but to stimulate him to consider what he does think. This is at least consistent, it seems to me, with the approach one uses as a counsellor with individual clients and as a training leader with groups of counsellors.

But such an approach may, I fear, puzzle or possibly challenge any reader whose training and experience rest on exact knowedge, established techniques and authoritative advice. I feel I must justify this different approach (and invite his indulgence) by explaining that personal counselling is concerned with aspects of human experience which are not precise, unequivocal, evenly progressive, intellectual or rational. People with personal difficulties (whether they are clients, counsellors, professional experts, trainers or authors) are, at that time and on that subject, confused and bothered, agitated or discouraged, angry, bewildered or fearful, and often the object of conflicting aims and feelings. There is nothing neat and tidy, technical, formal or precise about this. To present the reader with a neat and tidy guide to counselling, therefore would be as irrelevant as it would be attractive.

For the experienced caseworker, counsellor or student in training, this book is offered as a bridge between theory and practice. It is intended to help him in the lifelong task of finding his own orientation in the rewarding and disturbing field of personal relationships. No counsellor can ever claim that his training (in this sense) is finished – least of all those who train others or write books for them.

It is, I believe, consistent with this approach to use for illustration a short interview that has been transcribed from tape. This has been placed towards the end of the book because a consideration of what occurs in it makes better sense once the general orientation has already been explained. It is not offered as a typical or ideal interview, but has been chosen to give the reader an opportunity to consider his own thoughts and evaluations of a living exchange between two people, both of whom are trying to make sense of the difficulty confronting one of them.

In the end it is always the counsellor-reader's own values and judgments, his ability and skill, his compassion and constructive caring, and his perceptiveness, that determine the helpfulness of his interviews. That is why he (and not a technique) is the focus of these chapters.

The book is divided into two parts. Part I is concerned with the general orientation or theoretical framework within which counselling lies. Part II is concerned with what goes on in the process of this type of interview and the practical limits within which the counsellor works. A brief summary will be found at the end of each chapter.

Although the approach outlined here rests chiefly on the author's experience as a counsellor and in training others, he is indebted to many colleagues and consultants for much guidance and help in these two tasks. So far as books are concerned, I would like to record my indebtedness to each of those listed in the Reading List, which have stimulated ideas and experiments, particularly those by Professor Halmos, Bernard Steinzor, the classic *Emotional Problems of Living* and (not listed) Dr Michael Balint's *The Doctor, His Patient and the Illness*. The text is not encumbered with references. This is not out of ingratitude but because, as in counselling and in training others, I have learnt to work from life rather than from books, from experience rather than from theory. And if I may say this without impertinence, I would urge any counsellor to do the same. Books can throw much light on this subject but it is the subject that matters.

PART I

CHAPTER 1

Counselling and its Ideology

In its simplest terms, counselling may be described as a dialogue
in which one person helps another who has some difficulty that
is important to him. This will not serve as a definition because
it is oversimplified, as we shall see in later chapters. But it contains the elements of counselling, namely two people, a difficulty
of some kind, an interview and a purpose – to help.

Counselling is often, though not always, concerned with helping people to make a choice, come to a decision, make up their
mind. Hence the word is sometimes applied in commerce, where
we are offered a counsellor's services to help us choose the tele-
vision set, cosmetics, colour scheme or washing-machine that will
best suit our needs. To distinguish the subject-matter of this book
from aspects of salesmanship (or any other context in which the
counsellor has an axe to grind) I use the term Personal counselling. Of course a hair-do may be a very personal matter and so
may be a colour scheme. But the salesman, quite properly, is not
much concerned about *what* you choose as long as you choose
something. He would rather have a sale than no sale, whether
you can really afford it or not. From a long-term point of view
he would prefer you to choose something that will satisfy you
now and afterwards, because if you regret your choice and blame
him, you will not come back next time. So even his 'counselling'
is not totally impersonal. Indeed, some salesmen are remarkably
patient and listen to all kinds of marginal and personal considerations. Nevertheless, he has his own objective whereas a personal
counsellor is concerned with his client's objectives and interest,
not his own.

By the word Personal I mean here quite simply what anyone
means in ordinary conversation when we talk of a personal
problem or a personal matter. We mean that it is private and

individual and that it is of some importance to us. We sometimes imply that it is rather embarrassing to talk about, even though we very much want to talk about it. Many a good neighbour, friend or relation feels flattered but sighs inwardly when he hears someone say 'I have a personal problem I want to discuss with you'. He may be cornered at a party or on holiday or may be in a hurry. And he knows it will not be quick. Helping people to make up their minds and come to a decision on any personal matter cannot be quick and is often intricate, delicate and skilled. Hence the value of personal counselling even in making apparently ordinary, everyday choices. Friendly care and interest, and suggestions from somebody we trust are helpful. But more than this is often needed or we may get out of one difficulty only to stumble into another.

The difficulty may be not so much a question of making a choice or coming to a decision as of summoning-up the *ability* to choose or decide or put our decision into effect. This is why good ideas and suggestions are often useless. 'I know you are right but I can't do it. Why can't I?'

Sometimes the pressure of this situation is intense. Someone has reached a crisis in his personal life and is quite unable to deal with it, even if he knows how it should be dealt with. Knowing what to do is not the same as being able to do it. This conflict can arise in any area of his life – at work, at home, in social life, in marriage or being a parent – or it may arise from inside himself. He may have reached an intolerable stage of incompatibility in some personal relationship or, as it were, be quite unable to tolerate himself.

This may seem a far cry from making up one's mind about which carpet to choose for the sitting-room. But even this may sometimes become the focus of intense feeling, a battleground or the last straw. When we are (either as friends or in professional life) dealing with personal problems, particularly when these are problems of relationship, we may easily get into deep waters. Colloquially we tend to use the term 'psychological' for personal difficulties (whether of decision or of relationship) especially when they are of such intensity that they seem outside the range of ordinary reason and common-sense or friendly advice.

All of us who work with individuals (in whatever capacity) must be familiar with the psychological aspect of personal difficulties, using the word in this same informal way. Sooner or later we encounter someone who is reacting so strongly in a subjective, emotional way to his problem that it cannot be resolved by commonsense. Then we feel helpless or out of our depth. It is this which has led to an increasing interest in and demand for counselling of a skilled kind.

I must now amend the description given at the start of this chapter and say that counselling is a skilled dialogue in which one person helps another who has some personal difficulty that is important to him. In this sense, counselling may be called the practical application of the principles of casework, applied to a situation in which someone needs help of a personal (rather than a social or environmental) kind. And casework may similarly be described as the practical application of the principles of psychotherapy to the role in which the caseworker is functioning. We shall consider these connections more fully later on.

These innocent and elementary opening paragraphs represent the bare essentials of counselling, familiar enough to anyone likely to open this book. But for that very reason it is easy to neglect the impact that counselling makes in real life (compared with its impact in a book).

The first two elements were people, client and counsellor. Our training and our reading will have directed us to observe our clients, to put our eyes and ears at their service, to let them explain themselves and so forth. But what about the counsellors?

It is easy to think of them as being all the same, with a common pair of eyes and ears, and the clients as infinitely varied. But I know from experience that any such assumption is inaccurate. However fully or professionally trained, counsellors are not all alike. They are as varied as clients even though they sometimes talk their own characteristic language or jargon which may give an illusion of similarity. And what counsellor can, hand on heart, claim to have the same approach to every client? Or which of us can claim to be the same on Monday morning as we are late on Friday, or before a holiday or just after one? Counsellors, however well trained, are no more immune to the stresses of ordinary living than are clients. To read some of the requirements expected of them one might think they are a different order of being.

Counsellors are sometimes counselled not to tell clients what they must do or be but the experts and authorities do not hesitate to tell *them*. Such demands are well enough if offered as ideals. But if they are technical instructions then one has to ask how far in reality it is possible to fulfil them. For instance, one often hears counsellors say 'We *must* be non-directive'. When asked why, they reply 'We are told so in our training'. I do not think it is realistic to make sweeping and ambitious demands of counsellors or tell them they must be sensitive and adaptable and accepting. It is the trainer's business to make this goal easier of attainment, not just to preach it.

How does any counsellor see his task and his role – never mind how he is *supposed* to see it? This seems to me an important question because of its relation to the values each counsellor holds. I mean his assumptions about what is worthwhile, what is desirable, his norms of behaviour, how the work of counselling fits in with his own philosophy of life, his ideals. (Here and elsewhere I use the conventional 'he' to mean either sex.) If he cannot reconcile the work with his own values he will find it stressful in an unhelpful way. For instance, I have heard counsellors say 'Oh we never give advice, do we?' with an implied wink, as if to say 'We are not supposed to advise but really we sometimes do, don't we? Only we keep quiet about it.' Such jocular comments may sometimes hide a very real conflict of loyalty.

Such a conflict can only lead to inner confusion and make the work more difficult. To try to apply principles of counselling as though they are an authoritative technique is self-defeating, because applying a technique is impersonal and robs the relationship (with a client) of its vitality. It is the province of the counsellor to attend to the personal aspects of the difficulty that confronts him, but it is not a moral obligation on him. And he will be handicapped in this if he tries to split himself into two – a counsellor and his real self. He may be doing a particular job in a technically correct way but his sincerity will depend on how far his values as a counsellor are consistent with the values he holds as a person. If I can do so without offence, I would like to call this the white-coat syndrome. A counsellor may don a professional guise of uniformity. But there is a contradiction here in that one is trying to do an essentially personal job in an impersonal way.

I do not believe it is helpful to suggest that a counsellor's personal value-judgments should be kept altogether out of the work he is doing. For one thing, in moments of stress they cannot be kept out. For another, the attempt to keep them out means that he withholds part of himself from the interview. This, I fear, may sound like heresy to counsellors who (I am sure correctly) claim that one essential of counselling is that it is 'non-judgmental'.

The counsellor who is able to integrate within himself the ideology of counselling and his own personal value system will have no motive for being judgmental. He will not have to keep control of himself in order to avoid transgressing the ethos of counselling, nor will he need a disguise. He will simply get on with the job. If this seems like a gospel of perfection, perhaps one may put it this way: the more the counsellor's own value system is compatible with the ideology of counselling, the freer he will be to get on with the job, undistracted by internal conflict between what he feels like doing and what he has been told he ought to do.

Counselling, casework and psychotherapy are, I believe, based on assumptions that may be approximately listed as follows and which together comprise an ideology of counselling, both implicit and explicit.

1   Any individual is of intrinsic worth in himself, as a person. He is to be respected and not manipulated, exploited or used for any purpose. By virtue of his humanity he is entitled to such help and understanding as the counsellor can give him and to be accepted unconditionally, so far as this is possible.

2   Any person has a right to his own feelings and is not to be blamed for having them. Morality attaches to behaviour rather than to emotion. An exploration of what a person feels, in an uncritical atmosphere, helps to affirm his individuality and to clarify the relationships that are important to him.

3   No individual is independent of others. He has rights and obligations and so do they. The quality of his relationships with other people individually and socially is important for his and their well-being.

4   The quality of a person's relationships is not totally subject to rational control – it depends to a large extent on his previous experience of other people and on unconscious influences derived

from this. A client's characteristic responses to others will be reflected in his relationship with the counsellor and this provides both of them with an opportunity to understand more fully the limiting factors in his ability to make satisfying and satisfactory relationships with others.

5   The ability of a counsellor to be frank and undefended, uncritical and accepting during the interviews (that is, to shed his white coat) will largely determine how helpful he can be to the client.

6   The aim of counselling is to enhance the individuality of the client, to help him to extend his freedom of choice and decision while at the same time enlarging his sense of responsibility towards other people.

7   Moral injunction has no useful part in counselling though the moral aspect of any issues concerning the client or his situation need not be excluded from discussion.

8   An uncritical discussion of a person's inner feelings will help him to develop greater control over the ways in which he expresses them or acts on them.

9   The ultimate direction of counselling is towards helping a person to become both freer *and* more responsible, to live his life more fully, happily and creatively than he could before, and in fuller harmony with those around him.

These paragraphs are not intended to be a formal or final Nine Points or Declaration and I am not suggesting any counsellor should be asked to assent to them. Indeed, the thought of trying to get a committee of experts to agree on any such draft is truly daunting. What I am suggesting here, is that in a general and not precise way they represent some sort of common ground on which most counsellors would, I believe, agree as representing the ideology of personal counselling. The point of introducing them here is to consider how far a counsellor would in practice find them acceptable or in conflict with his own philosophy of life. His non-acceptance would not necessarily imply some non-ethical departure from the party line, indeed it might enable him to add or alter something in the conventional approach. Not all the paragraphs relate specifically to counselling : some are general, numbers 1, 2, 3, part of 4 and 8.

It is, however, one thing to give assent or dissent or suggest modification to general principles, especially if one is familiar with them; and quite another to consider them in the light of actual experience.

If we turn back for a moment to the elements of counselling at the beginning of the chapter we can ask ourselves what happens as the second person (the client) meets the counsellor and outlines his difficulty. Before he even opens his mouth he may already challenge the counsellor's acceptance of Point 1. He may look like the kind of person whom experience has shown to be untrustworthy; he may look shifty, crafty, devious and may instantly remind the counsellor of someone who cheated him or out-rivalled him. The counsellor may recognize the likeness or he may not. If he does, he will be able to explain to himself the intrusion of unworthy feelings. ('My God, he looks like that damned salesman who swindled us over the deep-freeze – talks like him, too.') But if he does not recognize the likeness he will just feel vaguely ill at ease, on the defensive or on the attack. For the moment at any rate, Point 1 tends to look like some pious piece of unrealistic idealism.

Then, after that interview, he sees a woman. She is bitter and extremely annoyed, she has had enough of it, it has got to stop, the counsellor must do something, it is entirely 'their' fault, she is blameless and if she doesn't get satisfaction, well. . . .

She too may remind the counsellor of someone, consciously or not. Why should she go on like this? How can he begin to make any sense of it unless she calms down and stops being self-righteous? Thinks: 'Oh Lord, yet another battle-axe with a grievance.' Most people (Point 2) 'have a right to their own feelings and are not to be blamed for having them' – but that doesn't apply to people like this, surely. She shouldn't be feeling like this, it is absurd and tiresome and unhelpful, even if 'morality attaches to behaviour rather than to emotion'. Self-righteousness (thinks the counsellor) is not good or praiseworthy : it is morally bad. Can anyone dispute that? And as for the rest of Point 2, if some counselling 'in an uncritical atmosphere (a what?) helps to affirm her individuality' well – in that case the less counselling the better, surely. But he brushes such thoughts aside and goes manfully (or womanfully) ahead.

His third client today is very different from those two. It is a father and he has come about his adolescent son. He is not angry nor has he a grievance. He has done all that could be expected of him and so has his wife. But the boy is heading for trouble, serious trouble, very serious trouble.

Unmistakably (and without reminding the counsellor of anyone in particular) this man is curiously self-sufficient. He is intelligent, capable, sensible and yet strangely remote. He does not seem to be really here, in the room. He is so clean, tidy, precise, calm and what he says makes sense. And yet it doesn't seem to concern him. Something obviously ought to be done about what he describes as 'the situation'. Perhaps he has been a counsellor or a social worker? No, that is not possible. He has been reading magazines or watching programmes about how people behave in certain situations. He is remote, detached. This man *is* an island. He is (if not totally, then very nearly) independent of others. His relationships with other people (the counsellor among them) are not important to him and his well-being is quite all right, thank you. It's just that his son is heading for trouble and it ought to be stopped. Point 3 seems no more applicable than the others. The counsellor sighs and greets his fourth client.

This is a very unhappy young woman. If anyone needs help, she does. She is withdrawn, helpless, lost, vague and dejected. She has a heap of troubles yet that is not surprising. She cannot meet you half way, even in an accepting atmosphere. You have to get through to her. She is pregnant again and wants another abortion but doesn't know how to set about it. Besides, there are other complications. . . . The counsellor is concerned and he begins to explore this young woman's history. It is an appalling history – mother's prostitution, father's drinking, slum conditions, beatings, locked in all day, stealing at a supermarket ('But I only took a few things'), remand home, approved school. What sort of relationships has this unkempt waif? You could hardly call it a relationship at all, in the interview. So this (Point 4) is the 'opportunity to understand more fully the limiting factors in her ability to make satisfying and satisfactory relationships with others'? (Thinks – You must be joking.) But how, exactly? Her lack of relationships (in any satisfying sense at least) may indeed depend on her previous experiences and not be subject to rational control. If it was, she would not be pregnant again. But having understood her 'limiting factors' where do we go from here? What 'opportunity' is there?

Perhaps there is no need to complete the list in any detail, since it is obviously the counsellor's unlucky day. But I must just mention how he reacted to a very arrogant and insulting client (Point 5). He felt on the defensive and critical and couldn't be as frank and accepting as usual. Then came a truly pathetic older woman who really just couldn't cope and never had. Indeed it was not possible to see just what individuality this poor shadow of a soul had, 'to be enhanced'. And as for her 'freedom of choice' ... (Point 6).

The seventh annoyed him. It was a young man who treated his children with appalling and callous cruelty. Never mind about counselling, this was too much. He got some well-deserved moral injunction. After all, it was nearly the end of a trying afternoon. The last client was very tense. The 'uncritical discussion' got going gradually but it led to such an outburst of desperate crying and anger that one could hardly help wondering what people outside must think. 'Greater control?' *She* lost it completely (Point 8).

That was the end of the afternoon's work. The counsellor left for home, wondering how many of today's clients he had been able to help towards a 'freer and more responsible' life and which of them he had helped to live 'more fully, happily and creatively than before' (Point 9). He stopped for a drink on the way, a little thoughtful.

In the bar are others whose work involves counselling in various contexts. One works with children and parents, another is concerned with old people; others with adolescents, students, teenagers, young people, the unattached. Some are professional caseworkers, one or two are voluntary part-time counsellors, others are counsellors in spite of themselves – that is to say, their work brings them distressed people as well as professional or vocational problems – a doctor, a clergyman, a health visitor. Our imaginary bar is quite a club. Perhaps the reader is, at least sometimes, to be found in there. For which of us, full time or part time, vocationally a counsellor or one by incidental necessity, has not at least metaphorically joined that company and been uncomfortably aware of a contrast between what we are expected to be and do and what in fact we are and do? To put it another way, which of us never suspects that the counselling white coat really belongs to the fairy-tale emperor?

I believe this situation is crucial to an understanding of personal counselling and to its successful (that is, helpful) practice. The failure to live up to the ideology needs to be taken seriously and not just dismissed as human frailty. To understand the factors that contribute to it will unlock the relationship between counsellor and client and release its helpful and constructive potential. It is all too easy for caseworkers and counsellors as well as the authorities who train them or write for them (including, of course, the present writer) to enter into an unconscious pact or conspiracy and deny the real nature of the interaction between helper and helped. I have come to this belief through a study of stalemate situations in which a counsellor feels he has done all that the books say or that he has been trained to do. He has built up a potentially useful relationship with the person who seeks his help but somehow can go no further. And in the groups with whom I work I find myself having to lead the discussion into a reappraisal of the very basis on which they have been trained. That is to say, the discovery by both them and me that they can make no further progress till they discard the white coat of professionalism.

This is not to suggest counsellors should go to the opposite extreme and engage in unprofessional relationships with those who seek their help. If we can only grasp the true nature of the problem that confronts us we shall find that a reliance on professionalism, technique or skilled role-acting is ultimately irrelevant and unhelpful.

To illustrate this point I would mention a curious feature of almost every new in-service training group I have ever taken. When it has become obvious that I decline the role of instructor or authority and offer my services simply as one who selects aspects of the discussion (or of the case under discussion) for a closer look, I often face a strong and sometimes hostile reaction. Some members resent this stance, feeling that if I am not prepared to teach counselling technique and indicate how the case should be managed, I am wasting my time and theirs. This reaction may be intense and the group find themselves with a heated and argumentative member who selects another member as antagonist. On other occasions some are at first confused and then gradually begin, as it were conspiratorially, to reveal holes in the white coat and confess to their transgressions against the ideology that has been expounded to them, usually to the benefit of the person they have been trying to help. Such groups, at this stage, have an opportunity of working together to puzzle this out, not just in theory but in any work problem that is today facing any one of them in which he is trying to make up his mind on how to proceed. That is to say, instead of seeking solace in that figurative bar, we can face up to the distinction between what we are actually doing and what we feel we are supposed to do or have been trained to do.

It may seem here that I am making sweeping and unsupported criticisms of the way counsellors are trained and the ideology that is, overtly or by implication, propounded to them. But that is not wholly so. Indeed, the problem arises not from the incorrectness or unacceptable nature of the tenets of the casework ideology but, on the contrary, from its rightness.

If one looks back at the nine points listed earlier in this chapter, the reader will still, I believe, find that they are not far from the basis outlined in any systematic casework or counsellor training. They may not be worded quite as he would like or as well as the orthodox books word them, and of course most of them raise marginal issues of a psychological and philosophical kind. But I do not think any authority who is today training counsellors or caseworkers would find any one of them wholly unacceptable or irrelevant.

And yet experience with people actually doing the work, in whatever field, forces one to the conclusion that, given the opportunity, any counsellor will find that it is quite impossible to live up to these ideals and indeed that only when he stops trying to do so can he make progress in particularly difficult cases. It would be easy to deduce from this that if counselling or casework theory is right, its practice is wrong, or vice versa. This, I think, gives many thoughtful casework practitioners and trainers a feeling of unease expressed by a constant inward-looking concern with what casework really is.

The counsellor who finds that he often falls short of the ideology he has been taught (and has accepted) need not despair. Nor need he be criticized. Indeed, his awareness of this tension may be a springboard for a useful step forward in his practical work. He need no longer strive to reach unattainable heights of professional technique. When a group of counsellors have accepted this (having first resisted it) they begin to approach their difficulties with a zest that gives their discussions a lively and constructive turn. But it is surprisingly difficult to break out of the belief that a personal relationship must be conducted along prescribed lines if it is to be helpful. In practice the reverse is true. To be effective, training should focus not on theory or even on technique but on developing the counsellor's perceptiveness, insight and constructive compassion. The problem facing the trainer is how to achieve this, how to make it possible. The unconscious pressure of accepted patterns of practice limits the freedom that is the counsellor's most valuable tool. That is why elaboration of theoretical principles can be misleading and restrict the practice of those very principles. This leads the counsellor (bewildered by a puzzling case or a demanding client) to search for explanations and technical devices by which he can extricate himself and his client from the impasse. But this will get him no farther forward. He can be helped only by the very approach he is being told he ought to use with his client, namely to try to see what the situation actually is, not how anyone ought to be behaving. Counsellors who would not dream of instructing their clients in how to be a success or run their lives, how to get on with authority, or a spouse or employer, or how to be more at ease within themselves, are sometimes urged to put their trust in books which (*mutatis mutandis*) do precisely this for them.

The ideological framework within which counselling takes place (its philosophy, so to speak) is no more than a frame of reference. It is most important that the counsellor should confront it with his own values, as was suggested early in this chapter. But to regard its principles and beliefs (for that is really what they are) as models which he, the counsellor, is obliged to copy in his counselling (whether or not he gives assent to them) is to ask for the stalemates I have described.

The counsellor sitting over his beer felt a hypocrite. He mistakenly believed he had to live up to the ideology as an imposed model, an unrealistic ideal. His initial reactions to those eight clients were not lamentable lapses of professional decorum but spontaneous reactions that make sense if only he can accept them. In any event, they may be of secondary importance in the interview because his primary task is to listen to what his client is trying to tell him. And even this is not a moral obligation or technical requirement, but follows naturally (if only it is allowed to) from the attempt to help someone who is in doubt or distress. One cannot know what the difficulty is except through listening and exploration, and the counsellor's initial reaction to the client is only important to the extent that it hinders this process.

However, the ideological issues are very far from side-issues for the counsellor once he is back in the bar, away from the dialogue with each client. Indeed, so important are they, in relation to himself and his work of counsellor, that throughout his career he will probably never have done with them, never (that is to say) have finally accepted or rejected them. The very perceptiveness or discernment that is the counsellor's only tool depends on being alert to the fundamental challenge presented to his own personality by someone whose problems and difficulties he is trying to illumine. A learnt technique helps him to start but does not carry him far. The very attempt to bring clarity into the situation of his client – so that both of them can see what is wrong and what is possible or impossible to alter – will be helped, limited or negatived by the relationship between them. But not only by that – it will be helped or hindered by the counsellor's own values and philosophy.

In essence, the counselling ideology rests on a tension between rigidity and flexibility, between dogma and discovery, between rejection and acceptance, between authoritarianism and creativity. The man or woman who believes that personal change is only possible through authority or manipulation and not through caring, sharing and discovery will never make a helpful counsellor because the work will be a personal threat to him. This he might discover for himself by matching his own value-system with such tenets as the nine points in this chapter. It is not necessary to accept them uncritically or absolutely. But if their general direction arouses a feeling of angry rejection, a wish to argue that they are wrong (rather than sometimes impossible, inappropriate or questionable) then the counsellor is unlikely to feel at home or be helpful in work of this kind. Sooner or later he would probably discover this for himself. But it is surely better to discover it before wasting too much of his own or other people's time in work for which he is not fitted and really, when it comes to the point, does not wish to be fitted.

People in difficulties can be helped in more than one way. There are personal and impersonal ways, and in a technological atmosphere the impersonal tend to be more popular. By definition, however, counselling is a way of helping people by personal means, not by impersonal authority or impersonal techniques. The counsellor is wasting time or energy in concerning himself with methods that are not available to him (because they depend on specialized techniques in which he is not qualified) and which in any event are only acceptable to those with an ideology of personal relationships that is incompatible with his.

Yet the discernment necessary to bring reality to light (as a joint discovery between one person and another) is so great a challenge that any sensitive counsellor will sometimes lack confidence, not only in his ability but also in the value-system within which he is working. Then inevitably he will hesitate before the personal encounter with the other person and hanker after an impersonal technique to rid him of the discomfort of a personal challenge. Thus in a book on counselling, recently published, one reads of conditioning techniques, aversion therapy and the like, and an experimenter who has apparently succeeded in making pigeons walk on tip-toe in circles in some Brave New Laboratory. What connection this achievement has with counselling is not immediately apparent but the manipulative ideology behind it certainly is. As an interpolation in a book on counselling it tells its own story. Perhaps I lay myself open to a charge of sentimentality if I find manipulative ideology repugnant, whether it is applied to birds, animals or human beings. I do find it repugnant, however, and as a counsellor I part ideological company from those who recommend impersonal techniques to remedy personal problems – always, of course, for the sufferer's benefit as judged by the expert.

Fortunately, counsellors do not have techniques at their disposal (though authorities who habitually think in manipulative terms allege that counselling is itself a technique). We cannot make our clients – or even pigeons – walk on tip-toe. We cannot even make them happier, more successful, more mature. Would we, if we could? I doubt it. As I understand our ideology, we would withdraw from *making* anybody anything. We are concerned with freedom, autonomy and the personal quality of relationships, not with expert manipulative techniques. The

assumptions about human relationships on which the counselling ideology rests are ultimately based on faith and on a value-
system whose fundamental tenet is respect for the individual.

SUMMARY

Counselling, impersonal and personal – application of casework principles
– the counsellor's own values – professionalism – nine assumptions in
counselling, casework, psychotherapy – limited control over inner feelings
– examples that challenge a counsellor – living up to the ideology –
stalemate situations – tensions between theory and practice – unconscious
pressure on the counsellor – listening and exploration – authority and
manipulative techniques – personal autonomy.

CHAPTER 2

The Context and the Counsellor

In the last chapter an attempt was made to explain the term counselling, so that the reader might consider its underlying ideology and compare or contrast this with his own value system or philosophy of life. Any reader, even though he works with people, may reject the concept as unreal or unacceptable, too vague, too permissive or amoral, in which event he is unlikely to read any farther. And there are plenty of social workers of the old school to whom counselling is wholly unacceptable. This does not prevent their being helpful in other ways, usually authoritarian or paternalistic.

If, however, he gives his assent to the counselling approach, the reader is likely to ask how far it is or could be relevant to his day-to-day task, and in what circumstances. This is what must be considered in the present chapter.

A convenient way to start is to invite the reader to ask himself how far and in what circumstances he can describe his role as that of a counsellor. The term means no more than one who, at that particular time and in a particular situation, is functioning in that way. It may be familiar to him or may be exceptional. He may feel it is the way he normally functions in trying to help people who consult him or whom he has to visit (or chooses to visit) for a discussion. Or he may feel it is not his normal province but is perhaps a method that can help where his usual way of working does not help or is not valid.

There is an important distinction here. For convenience I refer to 'the counsellor', but who is he? The role may be rejected by any social worker or anyone else in any work relationship, as was once expressed to me in the words 'It isn't counselling he wants but a kick in the pants'. Anyone who works in relationship to individual people in any helping capacity has to make up his mind what kind of help is indicated. That is to say, what is most useful bearing in mind all the circumstances, including his own predilection, his own abilities. This is not the detached expert diagnosing a situation, assessing a client and then prescribing the treatment of choice. He is himself a part of the treatment (if that is an appropriate term) and his reaction to the person before him and the situation under discussion is only part of it. The counsellor's personality, circumstances, training and normal role enter also into the choice.

Counselling differs from psychotherapy (using the latter term in its strict sense) in this respect. Psychotherapy is both a procedure or method of working, and it is a profession. One can be employed as a psychotherapist but one cannot be employed as a counsellor without further definition, such as student-counsellor, educational counsellor or marriage counsellor. There is thus no professional institute, association, college or school at which a counsellor can be trained and can qualify, though perhaps such a development is not far off. Therefore elements of counselling are absorbed and adapted into specialized varieties of training. But this skill is not well-defined, precisely because counselling itself is not the application of a technique or set of precisely enunciated principles. There is nevertheless, I believe, a general consensus not only about the ideology but also about the method. Anyone who works in a helping capacity with individuals can choose whether or not to make use of counselling in any particular instance. He does not have to put on a different hat. But he does make use of his relationship to the person in front of him in a particular way and for a particular purpose. He enters into a special kind of relationship with him. It is important to clarify this distinction because otherwise the relationship becomes confused and neither the counsellor nor the client knows what sort of relationship is evolving or why this is. The helper may offer personal counselling or, on the contrary, may confine himself to the technical, vocational or expert help that he has been trained to give. It is confusing both for himself and for the person he is trying to help if he is uncertain about these two roles or dithers uncertainly between them. With in-service training groups with which I am familiar I have often found it helpful, when someone describes a confusing and involved situation arising from his normal work, to ask 'What are you

C

trying to do?' This apparently naïve question is often difficult to answer, precisely because the member is uncertain which role he is trying to fulfil, either counsellor or whatever his profession or vocation may happen to be. The two are usually different, though not incompatible, and the choice is one that is made through a complex set of considerations, seldom simply and rarely objectively. The worker's own choice and his reasons for making it are important factors.

Perhaps the simplest way to illustrate this distinction is the question 'But what do you think I *ought* to do?' How is one to answer? Most people in the helping professions are confronted with it and may find themselves saying 'As a doctor (or whatever it may be) I would recommend so-and-so, but man-to-man I think so-and-so'. Or 'This is not a question that I can answer with certainty as your tutor (or whatever). It is not an educational question' and he may add 'Go and discuss it with your wife, your employer, a friend, your parents, your youth leader, student-counsellor, welfare officer, the chaplain, the doctor' – or whoever seems most appropriate.

This situation is extremely common, not only in the professions but for instance in the work of the Citizens' Advice Bureaux, with which I also have some experience. At its simplest, one may give as an example the question 'How can I get an abortion?' (or, say, a divorce). When the information has been given, comes the question 'Do you think I ought to?' This is a question of a different order. Like the doctor who says 'This is not my province' so the C.A.B. worker may reply 'It is really not for me to say what you ought to do, only to tell you how you can get this if you want it'. Then arises the question – whose task is it to advise anyone what they ought to do? Few professional advisers in these enlightened but uncertain days will undertake to give moral guidance to anyone else or, if they do, they will be scorned as unprofessional, and I believe quite rightly. Any professional person tells those who ask for his advice what they ought to do within the limits of his specialist competence. But there remains the 'ought' that is no one's province. Ought one to divorce one's spouse, if one has the grounds; ought a girl to have an abortion if it is available? One can get advice as to what remedy is available in certain situations but not as to whether one *should* adopt it or not. I recall with joy the comment of a doctor I once consulted over some trivial symptom that arose in far from trivial circumstances of my own making. 'It is not a doctor you need,' he told me, 'but a keeper.' However, this did not prevent him from relieving the symptom I complained of. The rest he left to me. Where one's client or patient is capable of dealing with his problem (that is to say, his personal choices or dilemmas) many an adviser draws this distinction. 'I can tell you how to cope with this', he says, 'but it is for you to choose whether you go on causing it.'

These situations are an everyday occurrence in the work of any general practitioner. He develops his own way of dealing with them, saying (quite rightly, surely) that medicine is not so much a science as an art. Any educated person today knows that mind and body cannot be so clearly differentiated as was once believed, knows too that each entity reacts on the other though perhaps in ways that are not yet wholly clear. One does not need to be medically trained to know that sometimes an unhappy marriage or uncongenial work can be a causative factor behind some bodily symptom, as can greed, ambition, frustration, guilt or grief. Perhaps non-medical people today find it less easy to accept the reverse and acknowledge the extent to which an incipient illness or some physical condition or handicap may disharmonize a close relationship – quite apart from the impact of mental illness.

There are similar divergencies of role with other professions besides the medical. How far, for instance, is a teacher or tutor concerned merely with the transmission of knowledge and the development of skill? How far is he also concerned with (to use an antiquated term) moral or ethical guidance? 'But do you think I *ought* to?' asks a student or sixth-former. Sometimes the tutor throws counselling to the winds and exclaims 'Oh no, of course not' (adding guiltily), 'since you ask me'; or alternatively maintaining the counselling stance in spite of himself, and asking 'Why can't *you* decide?'

To those who are religious, the clergyman may seem the best refuge in a moral dilemma. But which of the clergy today are so sure of their ground as to accept with equanimity the role of moral arbiter? Like anyone else, they know that morality is meaningless except on the assumption of personal freedom or (if that is overstating it), that moral choice is effectively limited by the ability to carry it out. There is no point in telling anyone what they ought to do (however sure of our ground we may be) if they cannot do it.

How is a solicitor to answer the same residual question ('But do you think I ought to?') when he has explained the legal position and outlined what is and what is not possible? Like the others, he can only choose between saying that this question lies outside his terms of reference or offer his services as a counsellor. What he and they are unwise to do is to advise on the basis of 'Well, speaking as man-to-man, if I were you. . . .'

This choice occurs in any profession or vocation in which people's emotions are involved. It may arise unexpectedly in what at first seems an impersonal or technical problem, involving only accurate assessment and expert opinion or advice. In practice the question is not so much 'Is counselling necessary to enable expert advice to be acted upon?' – it is more a question of 'Am I able and willing to enter into a personal relationship with this individual to help him sort out that part of his difficulty that lies outside my normal professional expertise?' This question does not demand an objective or technical assessment so much as a recognition of personal need, and a willingness and ability to try to meet it on the foundation of a truly personal relationship. This may well be as taxing (and as unfamiliar) to the worker as to the one who seeks help. One of the aims of this book is to enable the reader to accept the implications of this choice and to show ways in which, if the choice is made for counselling, it may best be undertaken.

In any of the personal service professions and vocations there will be men and women who dismiss counselling as irrelevant, saying perhaps 'I am only a . . . and it is not my business to get involved in the personal lives of those I am trying to help'. But there will also be those who make the opposite claim, saying 'If I don't do what I can to help with his personal problem, my other help may be useless or irrelevant', or 'If I don't help over this aspect, who will?'

As soon as one begins to acknowledge the need for personal help of the kind implied in such questions as 'Which ought I to do?' or 'Why can't I be different?' or 'I know I should, but how can I?' (whether or not one undertakes the task of dealing with it), one begins to see how widespread a need it is. It is only

fair to warn any reader considering counselling for the first time
that once he begins to be alert to this inner, personal need, he
will find it in places where he previously never suspected it. And
the more sensitive he becomes to this need, the greater will be
the demand on him to meet it. 'Go and see so-and-so' (his clients
or patients or students will say), 'he is someone you can really
talk to, he really tries to understand.' Some of us are willing to
do this, some of us are not. Most of us are willing sometimes but
not always, excusing ourselves on grounds of available time, vocational terms of reference or what we were trained to do. It is
always best to choose knowingly if one can. I recall a very
experienced barrister who said to me 'I know nothing at all about
human nature and I don't want to know anything about it. It
only confuses everything.' He was a warm and friendly person
just the same. He chose and he knew he had chosen. I recall a
physician who told me 'I don't want my patients to tell me what
is wrong. They always get hold of the wrong end of the stick.
It is for me to find out what is wrong with them by examination.
That is what I have been trained to do. The less they say the
better.' He too had made his choice.

In training-groups of professional people, this is an area that
needs to be explored circumspectly. Medical and legal practitioners are conventionally guarded about their relationship with
their clients or patients, so are social workers. This is not only a
matter of professional ethics, in which one does not divulge the
confidences of those who come for consultation, since this form
of training does not depend on detailed case histories but on
revealing what impact the person or case makes upon oneself.
No, the jealously guarded doctor-patient or solicitor-client or
casework relationship (which may be paralleled in any other
profession) is an area from which, as it were, outsiders are warned
to keep off the grass. However, a relationship between persons is
no respecter of professions. Indeed, the more experienced and
highly-trained an expert may be, the harder it is for him to
recognize that in the counselling or relationship aspect of his
work he is on the same basis as the beginner. It is a totally
different area of life. Expertise in some other field will not be
automatically carried over into this. It is a truism that disease
is no respecter of persons. It is just as true that personal difficulties are no respecters either. Anyone, however eminent, may get

appendicitis or a marital problem. But somehow it is usually easier for a marriage counsellor to accept that he has the one than it is for a surgeon to admit he has the other.

At this point, in our consideration of whether to embark on counselling or not in any particular instance, it would be as well to consider some of its practical requirements. The question of one's own attitude towards the general counselling ideology must now be replaced by asking how far the practical demands make counselling feasible.

The following, I believe, represent some of the basic requirements of any serious attempt at a counselling interview :

First, privacy. The dialogue must not be overheard nor must either of the two people feel that it may be. Audible voices in an adjoining room will make spontaneous discussion of deeply-felt issues almost impossible. To be seen by people walking past a window or a glass partition is equally putting-off. To be interrupted by telephone, secretary, innocent intruders, children, nearby church bells or pneumatic drills also makes an effective interview almost impossible.

Second, it is best for there to be only the two people present, counsellor and client. Sometimes a student is introduced and it is claimed that it has no inhibiting effect. But how does one know what a client never dared to say in front of this third person? If it is decided to have a third person present, he should be introduced, his presence explained and permission obtained. He should then take no part in the discussion unless asked but sit quietly (without writing notes) where he can be seen but does not have to be seen.

Third, counselling works most effectively when there is no intrusive difference of status between the two people, for example by the counsellor sitting behind a large desk or in a higher chair than his client or in any other way exhibiting symbols of superiority. I recall a psychiatrist who told me he found difficulty in interviewing a guardsman because he prefaced every remark with the refrain 'Permission to speak, sir?'

Fourth, counselling can never usefully be hurried. Less than half an hour is usually pointless, more than an hour exhausting and repetitive. The time available should be agreed at the beginning.

Fifth, many (though not all) authorities on counselling advocate 'neutral ground' for the interviews. That is, if possible not in the home of either party, nor in any office identified with any other role. This is perhaps a counsel of perfection and most counsellors have to work in their room or office that is used for other purposes.

Sixth, all the more reason, then, for the dialogue to be unofficial, informal, unstructured, spontaneous. Trappings of one's other role may well be put out of the way where possible. The atmosphere should be reassuring rather than forbidding.

Seventh, the counsellor will have to keep an eye on the time without rudely or intrusively doing so and should arrange a clock or watch with this in mind.

Eighth, the general conduct of a counselling interview rests on helping a client to express himself, to discuss alternative possibilities, to see what his situation, problem or difficulty means to him and to find ways by which he can more successfully cope with it. The more a counsellor has developed his perceptive skill the more helpfully he will be able to link one issue with another and the more uncritically he will be able to help his client acknowledge thoughts and feelings that are relevant to his predicament but which perhaps he has not expressed or acknowledged before. As is well known, the counsellor's first task is to listen attentively and (so far as he can) uncritically. He may then take the initiative from time to time in exploring more fully what certain issues mean to the person confronting him. Where he can, he will offer new ways of looking at the situation, exploring its meaning to the client in terms of his aims and difficulties, and at times will tentatively suggest new ideas or lines of approach, but always tentatively, so that they may as easily be rejected as accepted.

These eight points are not intended to be rules for the conduct of a counselling interview. I do not think many counsellors or caseworkers would disagree with them, so far as they go. They are offered here (as the nine points of ideology were offered in the last chapter) to help the reader to compare his own habits and way of interviewing. Where these differ he may like to ask himself how far a counselling interview seems alien to his normal method of working, why this is and how far these are mere habits or simple matters of taste or, on the contrary, how far they imply a difference of aim.

It would be tempting to visualize a busy counsellor in the press of a hectic day, dashing from one bit of his case load to another, in and out of the office, in and out of the car, reading the list just given. He might feel it is quite unrealistic or that counselling is not for him. If his interviews really must occur in very different conditions, useful counselling will be difficult. Sometimes interruption, noise, haste cannot be avoided, and sometimes the somewhat leisured, cool atmosphere outlined in these paragraphs may be inappropriate. For instance, in a busy, noisy, active youth club the skilled youth leader may seize an opportunity as it arises for a few words with one of his members and so open up a new relationship and reveal possibilities for counselling later. Such opportunities may be valuable where a formal invitation to a private discussion in the office might be brushed aside or rendered useless by embarrassed non-co-operation. Some of these questions will be looked at later, in Chapter 5. For the present we may return to the basic situation outlined at the very beginning, where one person confronts another with a problem or difficulty about which he wants help. Even here there may be exceptions in which it is the counsellor who takes the initiative and starts the discussion and the client may, at any rate at first, be unaware that he needs any kind of help or, indeed, may emphatically deny it.

Suppose, however, our potential counsellor decides that here is an opportunity to embark on a counselling discussion. The context in which he attempts this plays its part in what he can expect to achieve. If he cannot fulfil any of the points just indicated as being characteristic of this type of work, it will be almost impossible to achieve anything. He will first have to try to bring about the right opportunity, perhaps suggesting simply that on a suitable occasion the two of them might look into the problem more fully. Pressure of time often means that one has to put aside some special period for these interviews, after hours perhaps, at the end of a busy surgery or on some occasion when a youth club or home, hostel or school is quieter and free from interruption.

Another aspect of the context is the problem of dual loyalty. For instance, a sister tutor in a training hospital will frequently encounter a student nurse who feels driven to throw her hand in, give notice and get out into some other training. This situation, common enough in nursing training, also confronts tutors in universities, technical colleges, training colleges and similar institutions. Only through counselling will it become possible even to glimpse what the problem actually is. It will initially be laid at the door of some immediate incident, but if the student has the opportunity and is given the help to expand on the whole situation quite other factors are likely to emerge, such as anxiety about a parent or boy or girl friend, or about pregnancy or an unhappy love relationship, or a feeling of unpopularity, loneliness or failure in relation to fellow students, or a dislike or fear of the institution as a whole or some or all of the teaching staff.

The tutor acting as counsellor in such a context finds himself caught between two loyalties. I remember a sister tutor telling me that students in her care were deeply upset by the rigorous unfeeling discipline with which a particular ward sister controlled them. How could she help them to air their resentment, in order to get it into proportion and learn to cope with it, except with a feeling of guilt in apparently taking sides against a colleague in the same institution? 'I've been a ward sister (she said) and I know what it's like.' I have heard many difficulties of a similar kind from student-counsellors in secondary education and training establishments of various kinds. Sometimes the tutor has recognized only too well the attitude against which his students are rebelling. This may relate to a colleague he meets daily in the senior common room or to the principal or matron or indeed the whole organization and the way it is run. His counselling then feels subversive and he himself feels guilty. This situation may be intensely difficult and it is easy to take either of two courses. Either to call a halt to the counselling and let the student cope as best he may on the grounds that the counsellor is a part of the institution and a colleague of those who are complained of and cannot therefore be expected to continue. The alternative, and perhaps more courageous course is to tackle the colleague oneself. Such intervention may occasionally be justified but it is better avoided because it does nothing to help the individual student come to terms with reality. In practice, too, those who are unfeelingly or unjustly treated are often unconsciously a causative factor in the treatment of which they complain. Counselling may help to bring this to light and so make it amenable to modification or control. Taking up cudgels on behalf of the student would not achieve this or even make it possible. I have often met instances of this kind in in-service training groups, where a counsellor has been active on behalf of a student out of sympathy and a misunderstanding of his role. If such a course is thought about and chosen deliberately, such intervention may at least ease the strain on the student. But more often it is far from helpful and is deeply resented by his colleague, leading the counsellor to take sides more emotionally and still less effectively. The reason for this impasse can usually be found by patient discussion. What has occurred is likely to be some subjective factor in the tutor's make-up that, without his realizing it, is leading him to fight over again some battle from his own past experience that was never fought out to a conclusion. If that is indeed so, then his attitude to his colleague will not be a co-operative one and will be resented, leaving the counsellor more convinced than ever that the man (or woman) is hopelessly out of touch with students and should not be allowed to have them under his care. That might conceivably be true but is a conclusion that does not help the student or the counselling.

Other counsellors face conflicts of loyalty of other kinds. I have met child care workers who in certain cases are torn between their heart and their professional duty or feel themselves pulled by two opposing forces, the punitive reaction of magistrates or others towards parents who treat their children badly or incompetently, and the therapeutic approach that recognizes the ineffectiveness of punitive measures and the need for understanding and help. Anyone who works in any institution or organization that depends (as most have to) upon discipline will sooner or later find himself in the same dilemma. For instance, a youth leader may be torn between expelling a destructive or anti-social member from the club (because of his duty to his employers) or, on the contrary, overlooking a wilful offence because he knows the lad will not be helped by expulsion. Which is it to be, the individual or the club? In working with prison officers in a borstal I found acutely reflected the dilemma so widespread in society, whether to punish or on the contrary provide treatment for offenders. Probation officers too are frequently poised between the two arms of a similar dilemma, the individual's good or the well-being of society.

It is not uncommon today for someone to be appointed to the role of student or school counsellor, with or without special training. Such an appointment, especially if it is new, may be unexpectedly difficult to fill not simply because of the severity of the students' problems but because of an ambivalent or hostile attitude of colleagues towards the counsellor. For instance, some university lecturers resent the intrusion of a specialist with this new-fangled name of counsellor since they feel they themselves are perfectly capable of dealing with any student problems as they have always been accustomed to do. They may then openly or covertly steer students away from the help available through the new appointment until a truly intractable situation arises with which the tutor has struggled in vain. Now he brings in the counsellor to see what he can do. This is the equivalent of the well-recognized phase of any tutorial training group in which the first few cases brought into the group for discussion are so hopeless that no one could possibly get anywhere with them. Indeed, if the leader or any other member of the group offers any new suggestion or constructive possibility, this is shot down as impossible or as having been already tried and found useless. Counselling always involves treading on delicate ground that is emotionally charged, which is why it is so difficult and requires patience and skill. A newly-appointed student-counsellor may expect to find his presence not openly welcomed by colleagues but regarded with jocular ambivalence such as 'Ah, welcome to the counsellor who will solve all our students' problems'.

In other words, before counselling starts, there is already a potential web of expectation and prejudice, hope and resentment, conflicting loyalty and ambivalence, arising from the context in which it is placed. Unfortunately no training scheme can provide for this in advance because the factors contributing to it are so complex and varied that they cannot be foreseen. And, moreover, even if they could be foreseen they cannot be managed until they arise. It is no more possible to prescribe to counsellors how they should tackle such complications than it is to give new students a course of instruction that will enable them to avoid the many crises implicit in their development. A book can only provide an indication of these factors so that the reader may find guidance when the situation arises. That is why this book was described as a bridge between theory and practice in the realm of counselling.

SUMMARY

Counselling not a vocation of itself – a special kind of relationship, not a procedure of diagnosis and treatment – personal and technical help in various professional roles – the doctor, teacher, clergyman, solicitor, social worker and others – recognition of personal need not limited to any one profession – eight basic requirements for a counselling interview – privacy, two participants, equality of status, unhurried, neutral ground, informality, watching the time, attentive and perceptive listening – counsellors sometimes take the initiative – special sessions – dual loyalties – intervention on behalf of a client – relations with colleagues – expectations of a newly-appointed counsellor.

CHAPTER 3

The Dialogue

In this chapter the word Dialogue is used in order to emphasize that the exchange between counsellor and client is mutual, in a way that is not conveyed by the more usual term Interview. Most interviews are largely concerned with eliciting information. The relationship therefore tends to be one-sided and the two people are not truly colleagues of equal status, although they co-operate. In counselling, they *are* colleagues working on a project that concerns both of them, even though the problem is brought by one of them. Each makes his own contribution to their joint enterprise. The client knows more about his situation than the counsellor knows. But the latter brings to the discussion his own skilled contribution, the perceptiveness and discernment arising from his ability, experience and training. He sees more possibilities in the situation than his client can, both because of these qualifications and because the person consulting him is subjectively involved, and possibly overwhelmed in a way and to a degree that the counsellor is not.

We come now to consider this dialogue on the assumption that the person acting as counsellor is sufficiently in sympathy with the approach to make the attempt. He has also, of course, to be sufficiently in sympathy with the person he is about to help. The very concept 'help' suggests this, but it is also something of a pitfall. To give help is the avowed purpose of the meeting, which is not simply a sympathetic or social conversation. There is an implied outcome. The participants should understand better at the end of it the nature of the difficulty that confronts one of them. They will have begun to see helpful possibilities that were not apparent before, as well as seeing difficulties that were inherent in the situation but were perhaps ignored or evaded. This is not merely to provide a solution to a problem, as in an advice column or panel game. It is to help someone appreciate more fully what his difficulty is, how he himself is involved in it and what it means to him – not just out of interest or sympathy, but with the specific aim of helping him to cope with it more effectively, realistically and responsibly, that is to say more freely, less compulsively or blindly.

But this situation of helper and helped carries overtones that need to be considered in relation to working as colleagues. Why does anyone act as counsellor? This is a difficult question. Some of us, fearful of sounding smug and perhaps to disarm criticism, profess disreputable motives – manipulating others, being inquisitive, outwitting authority, getting the better of the establishment. But perhaps no one can answer with certainty, for which of us can be sure of his own motives?

The purpose of such self-examination is to keep our objective within reasonable bounds. For instance, if we tell ourselves that we want to help our clients to become more mature, we may reflect on how far this is realistic or even possible. We may find we are aiming to change people according to standards that we (but not they) take for granted, standards that we regard as absolute but which they regard as merely conventional.

By what right do we offer to help others and what kind of help do we envisage? The very concept of helping can be a barrier to successful counselling. There is a slightly irritating paradox in this. The more we try to help, the less we succeed. The lighter we can sit (as it were) to the overall aim of being helpful, the more likely we are to be so. Two issues are involved here. The first is that counselling becomes self-defeating if one adopts an active, zestful, manipulative approach – 'I'll help him if it kills me'. The second issue is more subtle. To be the helper in the dialogue is to be on the side of the angels, to don a white coat not as a uniform or professional badge but as an angelic robe.

If this strikes the reader as unduly cynical, I am sorry. But there is worse to come. I have often heard trainee counsellors make such observations as these : 'It is not the student but the parents who need counselling', 'It is not the wife but the husband who needs help', 'The problem would disappear if only one could get at his tutor and counsel *him* – that is the cause of the whole thing', 'I went to see the father to counsel him, but he refused to see me – so there is nothing more to be done'. These remarks suggest an aggressive approach, implying that counselling is something you can do to people (either for their benefit, or for someone else's or for the general good). But it is not a technique that can be used on people whether they wish it or not, even for their own benefit. Many people find this view difficult to accept. However, personal relationships are different in kind from impersonal, non-personal, technical or functional relationships and cannot be forced without being destroyed. I disagree fundamentally with those who claim that counselling is simply another form of conditioning. This view arises from blindness to the interplay (both conscious and particularly unconscious) between two personalities who have a value relationship with each other. (It is not necessarily a loving, friendly or co-operative one – it may be hostile or even destructive.)

The concept of helping inevitably carries a good connotation. 'I am the helper, you are the helped. I offer you my help, refuse it at your peril. I know what you need better than you do. I can enable you to do what you cannot do without me.' It is not easy for counsellors to avoid an implied aura of the guardian angel who has been trained in some celestial college to help poor, fallible, suffering mortals here below. And, may I dare to say, there is sometimes just a whiff of psychological or professional sanctity in casework training, just a suggestion of 'more mature than thou' or of our unconditional love for our clients. Actually it cannot be unconditional for it depends on their being willing and able to accept it. And it depends also on the counsellor's ability to accept his client.

Perhaps it is inevitable in a co-operative effort such as counselling that one has a feeling of regret if a potential client is unwilling or unable to co-operate. Sanctity apart, a counsellor cannot avoid a certain sadness if the opportunity for a joint effort to help his client is rebuffed, because he can see the potential value in such an undertaking. But that is not the same as feeling injured.

The importance of this issue is this. Sometimes it is essential that the person being helped should be free to express hostility to the counsellor. We shall consider this more fully later, when we come to consider the client rather than the counsellor. For the present it is important to appreciate what happens if the counsellor does (more correctly, the extent to which he does) see himself in the wholly beneficient light I have been suggesting. It is unrealistic and limiting. Many a client wants to express hostility not just by describing it but exhibiting it, living it, venting it. Indeed, this is a vital part of counselling. It is denied if the counsellor insists on being the good, loving person and cannot enter into the experience as a real person but sits aloof and says 'That makes you feel angry'. Counselling is often more effective if the counsellor comes off a non-directive pedestal.

Collectively, one may see this same problem reflected in the passionate defence of the so-called voluntary principle in some organizations. It is certainly worthy and commendable that people should take trouble and spend time (and often be out-of-pocket, too) on voluntary service to help others. But when it comes to a passionate refusal to consider being paid or even reimbursed for expenses, when it comes to an assumption that those who earn their living in any helping profession are somehow not quite so pure in spirit as the volunteer, but must be a bit base, callous, case-hardened or besmirched – then surely it is time to examine the implications. (The salaried helpers return the compliment by referring to the volunteers as do-gooders, half-trained amateurs or busy-bodies.) It took marriage guidance counsellors thirty years to accept payment for their difficult and painstaking work. Even today scarcely five per cent accept any payment at all. However, they are not the only voluntary workers, doing a skilled job, who fight fiercely to avoid being paid for their efforts. Sometimes it seems people will defend to the death their right to be 'more voluntary than thou'.

For many readers this will be a side-issue, since their counselling will be done, so to speak, in the boss's time and as part of the work they are normally doing. Others may be employed as counsellors. The arguments about payment are an expression of a deeper concern implicit in the concept of one person helping and the other receiving help, not with an external problem but in his personal life, his emotions and his close relationships. The normal process by which the two participants begin to sum each other up will inevitably contain some element, on the counsellor's part, of assessing the other's willingness to be helped. That is reasonable since sometimes counselling may not be the way by which they can best be helped. We shall consider this aspect later.

The initial assessment of the client's ability to be helped can easily be confused by a rather different consideration – whether the client accepts his role of recipient and that of the counsellor as giver or expert. Most counsellors prefer their work to be free from any question of giving or withholding money or material aid. I have heard child care workers complain that this issue makes the counselling aspect of their work more difficult, as well it may. They are put into the position of giving or withholding, and their clients respond accordingly. Some psychotherapists say that the question of fee is an unwelcome complication to the relationship with their patients, while others maintain that it is good for the patient to pay.

Perhaps the reality of the terms on which counsellor and client confront each other could be summed up like this : 'Let us, if you agree, look at the difficulty that concerns you. I have a certain kind of help to offer but I do not know how useful it can be to you. Perhaps we can usefully combine our two points of view of your situation to see what you can do about it.' That sounds rather stilted and I do not, of course, suggest anyone would express it in quite those words. But it does present the elements of the dialogue at its outset, at least from the counsellor's angle. The other may, naturally, see it differently or be confused as to what can be expected from the discussion.

Before going on to consider other aspects of the dialogue we must distinguish three different circumstances in which the meeting may occur. It may be at the request or demand of a third party, at the suggestion or invitation of the counsellor, or at the request and on the initiative of the client. These three categories will affect the way the two people see each other and may set limits to what can be reasonably expected from their meeting. It is obviously not helpful if the two of them are at cross-purposes about the nature of their discussion. And the counsellor may inadvertently be subject to pressures that arise from outer circumstances over which, initially, he has no control.

Sometimes, then, an adult or young person is sent to see the counsellor. He may be compelled to go (as in a school, borstal or prison for example, or in any of the armed services, where he is instructed to go and see the padre or welfare officer).

D

He may then certainly not view the counsellor as being in a helping capacity and may not even be willing to discuss the problem. He may come reluctantly and in a hostile or truculent frame of mind. The counsellor may resent this but has to accept it. He may feel some doubt about the reasons for sending the client as in the situation I described earlier, in which a tutor or lecturer or head of department disapproves of the appointment of a counsellor and regards it as an intrusion on his territory, or even as an insult or a slur on his ability to deal with his students' problems. Even voluntary counsellors may find themselves with a client who has been sent by someone else, his wife perhaps or his doctor or solicitor, employer or manager who has tried in vain to deal with the problem. Sometimes a referral may be made from some high quarter where one is anxious to make an impression, or from someone who is known to be critical of the whole idea of helping by discussion. The counsellor may then see the referral as a challenge to prove the effectiveness of his role and this will interfere with the spontaneity and mutuality of his task.

These considerations make the basis on which counselling can begin at least ambiguous. For whose benefit is it to be? In our original description of the elements of the counselling situation we included the words 'important to him'. That is to say, a client to whom the personal aspects of the situation are not important or who is indifferent to the outcome cannot be helped by this method. Here one may have to distinguish indifference from a defensive pose, adopted because the situation is too painful or humiliating to be faced openly. Usually the latter state of affairs will be betrayed by a hint, if one is only alert and perceptive enough to notice it and appreciate its implication. Any counsellor who is unfortunate enough to receive a run of this type of referral may begin to suspect a (perhaps unconscious) intention to prove that he is useless. Whether this is so or not, he is usually wise to explain to whoever sent the client that he can only be useful if the client is really willing to take part in a discussion of the problem. Those who are already prejudiced against counselling (and many people in positions of authority are critical of it) will take this sometimes as an admission of what they had long suspected, that the thing is a mere pretence. They sometimes say, 'If it only works with a willing person, what is the use of it? I can work perfectly well myself with those who are willing to accept my advice'.

Often, however, a frank willingness to abandon any attempt at counselling or discussion if the client does not want it, and an offer to end the interview at that point, brings about a change of heart. Naturally enough, the client may see the counsellor as another version of the very authority figure who cannot help him or even remotely understand what his difficulties are. And it is hardly surprising if he assumes the counsellor will operate in the same way. Therefore it may come as a surprise to find that he does his work in a very different way and is willing to listen and try to understand. The counsellor may then find himself in the dual loyalty situation I mentioned earlier, for the client may complain at length about the treatment he has received from whoever sent him along. To discuss this openly and frankly without taking sides is valuable but often difficult – especially when the counsellor feels the criticisms are justified. But it will not help if he aligns himself with the client against authority or against any individual with whom he is in an every-day working relationship. Instead of taking sides it is better to discuss how the client can deal more effectively with his problem, since any of us may find ourselves up against uncongenial people and it is no use expecting a counsellor (or anyone else) to change them.

Social workers sometimes find themselves in difficult situations of this kind. Those who have statutory powers or work in some official capacity find themselves caught in a web of rival interests and loyalties. For instance, someone trying to sort out a family problem where there is a brutal or neglectful parent may have to face the duty imposed by the magistrates or other authority, and also the hope of winning over or helping the parents. He also faces the painful conflict as to what is best for the child – to be removed into care or to endure further sufferings while attempts are made at counselling with either or both of his parents. Child care workers often have to carry such intense emotional conflicts that are inherent in work of this kind, as do N.S.P.C.C. staff, health visitors and psychiatric social workers.

With a reluctant or indifferent client counselling cannot begin at once and there may have to be several meetings or visits, often centred on practical, environmental concerns before it is possible to make a start. Sometimes the worker accepts an unconventional, uncongenial or unpromising set of circumstances in order to make any start possible. The resourcefulness and kindly patience of some social workers, biding their time and accepting rejection or hostility like so many saints, because they sense that counselling help is really wanted in spite of slammed doors, insults and evasion – all this is sometimes deeply impressive. And it works in the end, just because they shed the white coat and do not see themselves as saints or good figures, but simply use their ingenuity in the day's work and have faith in the value of the contribution they can offer. In some ways these situations are easier for them than for a voluntary worker because there is less pressure on them to be a good figure or helper. As one of them said, when involved in a specially taxing piece of work, 'Oh well, at least I get paid for it, so I don't have to be *good*.' Collectively, voluntary workers are sometimes liable to peculiarly bitter and hostile feuds of an intensity which perhaps arises from the strain of trying to be good, kind, helpers. Which of the large voluntary helping organizations has not been through an internal or external upheaval of almost lethal intensity? Then it all settles down after a few resignations or sackings and can return to helping again. Nevertheless, the stress and intensity of these human factors is a force to be respected and, at least in my view, is a powerful argument in favour of being paid for whatever useful work one can do. Those who cannot tolerate being paid can always do committee work where one can sometimes successfully be both aggressive and useful.

We must now consider the second situation, where the counsellor has taken the initiative and asked for or suggested the discussion. This presupposes an already-existing relationship, though this is not always with the person invited. For instance, any social worker who is in professional contact with one member of a family may seek an interview with another member. This is usually for some specific purpose, perhaps to get a fuller case history, to hear another point of view of the situation in order to complete the picture (since the worker only sees the client as he is now, whereas another member of the family can explain how he has changed). But these secondary interviews are not necessarily of a counselling character unless there are aspects that the second member of the family is worried about or wants help with. And in this situation the worker may be inadvertently drawn into being a go-between. This may be unavoidable but it is usually mistaken since it is preferable that people should be helped and encouraged to manage their own relationships, rather than for the counsellor to carry messages to and fro. This is a pitfall for marriage counsellors who may avoid a necessary confrontation between the spouses by trying to act as mediator, carrying messages from one to the other. Similarly a student-counsellor may offer to see a tutor or lecturer on the student's behalf instead of helping him to find a way of tackling the problem himself. Such intervention tends to make both counsellor and client feel that the former is a good, helpful figure but really it would be better to discuss with the client how it is that he cannot manage the situation more effectively himself. In counselling the aim is not to carry a client's burden for him but to find how he can carry it himself. Then he will become better able to deal with a similar situation if it arises again. But if we do the job for him he will have learnt nothing except where to come again next time. This is not tough or unsympathetic unless the counsellor both refuses to do the task on behalf of the client and also refuses to discuss with him how to set about it, how it has arisen and why he finds it difficult. A school counsellor who has been a teacher will be familiar with the distinction between doing something for a child or helping him to do it for himself. So will any parent.

The readiness with which a counsellor agrees to invite a third party to see him is often an indication that for internal (usually unconscious) reasons of his own he is getting drawn in as an advocate or agent rather than a counsellor. Most problems of relationship involve some kind of triangle (as we shall consider in a later chapter) and this applies to the counsellor as it does to his client. The client's situation may be echoed in the counsellor, and reflect some unsolved relationship from his own experience. By identifying himself with his client and his predicament he takes the problem into his own hands and tries to solve it by proxy.

But to approach a third party because the first asks one to, or because one wants to fight his battles for him or relieve his unhappiness, is quite different from approaching a potential client because one has noticed something that seems to need unravelling. This can be most helpful, especially to a shy, timid or anxious person who perhaps would not be able to summon up the courage to seek an interview even though there are facilities for doing so. I recall a moving incident of this kind described by a youth leader. He sensed that a member of his club was in trouble by observing a deterioration in his behaviour at the club and in his appearance. He knew the lad well enough to realize that he would shy away from a direct approach, however well meant. While this leader was still watching and waiting there was an expedition into the country where the lads could bathe, fish and play games. He noticed this particular member go off with his fishing rod, followed him and simply sat beside him and waited. Presently they got into conversation. Before long he was told about a severe problem that called for a great deal of patient and careful sorting out.

A similar occasion came my way from a woman teacher who noticed one of her sixth formers feel faint during a talk from a visiting doctor about sexual development. When this happened a second time the teacher realized there might be something going on in the background that called for her help and, like the youth leader, sought an opportunity rather than taking the bull by the horns and perhaps alarming the child still farther. In this instance too there was a very difficult situation, involving sexual promiscuity in the child's home. Such situations need the utmost circumspection, sympathy and tact if they are to be handled usefully. Probably most youth leaders, teachers and student-counsellors who may read this book will recall examples of the same kind. Here the counsellor or potential counsellor is taking the initiative but with discretion and sensitivity, not driven by an over-eager desire to interfere or by misplaced zeal.

The third situation is where the client approaches the counsellor of his own accord. His intention may not be what the counsellor expects nor what he welcomes. Many a marriage counsellor has been approached by a husband or wife who has taken the trouble to make an appointment and sometimes waited several weeks for it and has travelled a considerable distance only to explain that it is not he or she who needs counselling but the spouse, often indeed requesting the counsellor to make sure that the spouse is seen by a psychiatrist. Others on the contrary come openly asking for help in a situation that is getting out of hand and which they feel unable to put right. This may seem exactly the type of client a counsellor likes, since they can get down to work at once. Someone needs and wants help, has come to get it and has enough faith in the work to seek out a counsellor – even while saying (as many do) 'You are the last resort'.

Flattering as it is for the counsellor to have his function thus recognized, it may be something of a pitfall. Just because the situation so closely fits the counsellor's ideal in being recognized as a helpful figure, he may respond somewhat glowingly and without realizing it begin to assume that the spouse of such a sensible client must surely be the one who is causing the difficulty in the relationship.

Some willing clients, whether married or not, in any kind of circumstance and confronting any kind of counsellor, quickly get on to a friendly and co-operative footing, responding readily to the counsellor's attempts to listen perceptively and understand the difficulties. But if this client (who at first seems so easy and rewarding to work with) is a person who is rather specially dependent, he may begin to exploit the counsellor's good offices and gradually make greater demands. This can put any counsellor who has not spotted it into considerable difficulty. Gradually the time comes when the counsellor has to refuse what is asked or hinted at, and this may be bitterly resented. It is as though the initial stages of the counselling were a bit too easy for both of them, a rather too dependent client and a counsellor who was over-eager for results. These are the clients who are apt to be effusively grateful. It is pleasant to be thanked for one's efforts, especially if one is unpaid, and it makes the counsellor feel appreciated and useful and a good figure. But when the client's demands or appeals reach unrealistic levels and have to be declined, a difficulty faces them both. The counsellor has now to tolerate being regarded as a rejecting, unsympathetic figure and the client must face the unreal nature of his expectations. This can be too difficult for either of them. Then the counsellor deliberately or unconsciously brings the sessions to an end, sometimes saying it is in the client's interests that help should be sought elsewhere, since counselling only seems to be upsetting him. Or the client may take himself off, make a quarrel with the counsellor, become agitated or deeply resentful and feel he has been let down by the very person who seemed at first so willing to help.

This unsatisfactory outcome is very common and it is difficult for those who train counsellors to help them avoid it. That is why we have had to spend part of this chapter looking at the implications of being a good, kind figure. Ultimately, the counsellor is indeed a helpful figure and he has a valuable skill. But he cannot expect and should not be expected always to be a nice person in relationship to his client. It is sometimes extremely difficult to face first the grateful dependence and then the disappointed hostility of the client one is working with. Such phases are nearly always necessary before the difficulty can be got into proportion. Sometimes the pendulum starts at the other extreme and the counsellor faces hostility first and dependence later. Then he may be tempted to break off the meetings in the first stage, referring the client elsewhere or labelling him as too grossly hostile to accept help. Or he may keep going and as soon as the much more pleasant dependent stage is reached, feel that all is now well and there is no need to go farther. It is usually best to keep in touch (if circumstances allow it) until this pendulum has swung to and fro for quite a while.

In the first two instances (where it is not the client who takes the initiative) there are preliminaries to be sorted out before the counselling can really begin. The counsellor may, as it were, have to bide his time and await an opportunity. Or he may have to overcome (through explanation) the unreal expectations either of the client or the authority who sent him along. And at other times he may need to be ingenious and persistent merely to establish communication. When the client comes of his own accord there may still be these preliminaries, though they are usually quicker and easier. One may need to explain that it is not only the immediate crisis or problem that needs resolving but the wider and deeper question of how it came to arise. This is specially true when, as is so often the case, the actual problem presented to the counsellor as insoluble can be seen to be the outward expression of a relationship that at present cannot work harmoniously.

Once these considerations have been covered and an opportunity arises for a discussion of the predicament, the actual counselling may start. Some simple guidelines may be helpful. For instance, the actual facts in the situation are often far less important than one might suppose. Those that are important will emerge in the discussion. The counsellor is therefore wise to wait rather than begin by 'getting the facts straight' with a string of questions. If he does ask for details, he will find the balance of the exchange is upset and he becomes an interviewer rather than a counsellor. This is discouraging and disheartening to anyone who has difficulties that he cannot quite understand or master. And it may lead the client to feel, quite mistakenly, that they need not be faced at all. He has only to give correct answers to all these questions and then, presumably, the solution will emerge. This procedure is conventional in the functional or technical aspects of a situation but is totally unsuited to the personal, emotional or counselling part of any difficulty.

The counsellor is usually wise therefore to listen attentively not just to the factual problem but to the way it is expressed, the implications (often noticed because they are hurried over with the phrase 'of course'). He may be alert for mixed feelings and in particular observe the way the client sees him. It is often helpful to show that he (the counsellor) is interested not only in finding a 'solution' but in how the problem has arisen, what it means to this person in emotional terms, how far it is an expression of conflicting aims, wishes, feelings, ideals, values, how far it stems not from the factual frame of reference but from relationships to other people or even (if this is not too odd a way to express it) the client's relationship with himself. It has been well said that when a man describes his wife he tells you more about himself than about her. This applies not only to man and wife relationships but to any. It is the subjective side of a relationship that is important in counselling, how a person sees others (or one other), not whether they are really like that. Indeed, there cannot be objective truth in a relationship. The expert who claims to be able to describe a person objectively may assume that no feelings of his distort his objectivity. But if that is so, what sort of relationship is it? It is likely that he is ignoring the personal, emotional aspects of the client's life and concentrating on facts rather than feelings.

The object of training for counselling is not, I believe, to render the counsellor more objective in his relationship to those he is trying to help, though many authorities see it this way. In my view that is not helpful because it destroys the spontaneity and warmth of the relationship and gives the counsellor a feeling of superiority that is unjustified. Perhaps that is why it is popular. No, I believe the purpose of training should be towards developing a deeper sensitivity and emotional response to another individual, coupled with an increasing confidence and willingness to share one's reactions with him. So far as training can lead the counsellor to acknowledge the multifarious sides of his own personality, it will help him not so much to become more objective as more responsive. It will sharpen his discernment while at the same time increasing the warmth of his understanding. We shall return to this point later, when we come to consider the crucial question of involvement.

SUMMARY

Counsellor and client as colleagues – implications of being a helper – ability to deal with problems more effectively – objectives – clients who need to express hostility – part-time and incidental counselling – material help – clients who are sent – their reluctance or hostility – dual loyalty – statutory powers – clients seen on the counsellor's initiative – secondary interviews – the role of intermediary – clients who come direct – their expectations – dependence, gratitude – impossible demands – hostility – guidelines for interviewing – the purpose of training.

CHAPTER 4

Counselling and Psychotherapy

The foregoing chapters may be summarized as follows. Counselling is concerned with change and with values. There is no
absolute or precise ideal of wisdom, mental health, social equili-
brium or the Good Life to act as a clear goal towards which the
counsellor is trying to direct his client, only a hazy territory
compounded of all these, blurred at the edges and characteristic
of each counsellor and each client within their social context.
However imprecise, these issues are relevant and any of them
may helpfully enter into the discussion. But counsellor and client
have to discover their common ground. There are always limits
to what any counsellor or the process of counselling can achieve,
both in extent and in depth. It is therefore necessary for the
counsellor to be aware of limits and be willing to explain them.

Vague terms such as integrity, autonomy, stability, flexibility are
all very well as a general expression of the goal of counselling in
the abstract. But they are of little help in its practical work.
Indeed, one of the values of counselling is that it helps each
individual client to discover what it is that he wants, and what
he is getting in the way of realizing or obtaining it. Therefore
the counsellor helps him to discover what the problem, difficulty
or predicament means to him, and why he cannot find his way
through it, deal with it or accept it to his own satisfaction and
without undue conflict with others.

There are usually both external and internal aspects of
situations that disturb people. Some external change of circumstance has occurred. The client may have brought it about or,
on the contrary, it may have come upon him unawares and
without his having taken any part in it. Then comes his reaction
to this change of circumstances, which may be painful, difficult,

worrying, or frustrating in a way that he finds disturbing because he feels powerless to improve his situation unaided. Indeed, he will often explain that his efforts to surmount his difficulty or to accept the inevitable and adjust himself to it have only made matters worse, either for himself or others. It is usually an impasse of this kind that leads someone to seek a counsellor's help or to react in such a way that someone sees the need and offers help.

As we look a little more deeply into the relationship between any counsellor and his client we see more clearly how different it is from conventional ways of dealing with another person's problem. To express it negatively first : the counsellor is not an expert who examines, diagnoses and prescribes a remedy. He is not an authority who is in a position of power to give orders or instructions, involving penalties for disobedience or non-conformity. He is not an idealist pleading for adherence to a model and urging his client to greater efforts in attaining that ideal or modelling his life upon it. He is not a leader winning support for a cause or trying to urge a follower to greater efforts by appealing to his better nature, boosting his diminished self-confidence, offering rewards in some distant goal or playing on his anxiety or guilt. He does not bribe or cajole, threaten or appeal.

A counsellor does not operate in any of these ways. This is not because they are necessarily wrong or ineffective but because they do not fall within his terms of reference which we have considered already, that is to say, the personal, internal, emotional aspect of an individual client's confrontation with some predicament in his personal life. The counsellor (at any rate in that capacity) cannot change circumstances, though he may suggest ways by which the client himself can alter things for the better or find he can accept the inevitable. The counsellor is concerned with the impact of events on his client, his emotional reaction to demands, threats or opportunities. Most important of all, the counsellor is concerned with what the client is able or unable to do in order to adjust himself to the change or demand. This distinguishes counselling (and similar kinds of help such as case-work and psychotherapy) from more conventional attempts to remedy personal difficulties and problems by authority. Authoritative methods presuppose either that the client can do what he is told or advised to do or (if he cannot) that the adviser or authority has the means to make him. Reward and punishment, threat or promise, diagnosis and remedy, expertise, idealism, suggestion and appeal all presuppose that the client is amenable to such treatment. If he is not, something else has to be tried. These approaches are all authoritarian in that they depend on superiority of status, ability, expertise, technique, authority or power over the recipient. They are often effective for their specific goal, namely modification of behaviour or an increase in the well-being of the recipient as defined by the expert or required by those around him. Counselling differs from these methods in the mutuality of the relationship between counsellor and client. That is why I have referred to them as colleagues working on the problems or difficulties of one of them. It is a joint exercise in therapy. But it is not a therapy that one person applies to a docile other. It is a therapy that can only be effective on a basis of equality of status between the two of them. It is an examination of what the problem is and what it means to the client, how it affects him, and what he can or cannot do about it. The object is not so much to remove the problem at all costs as to enable the client to do what he could not do before. It is then for him to decide whether he wants to do this.

Critics of this approach sometimes say that counsellors tumble over backwards to maintain that they are not processing their clients, applying a technique to them, giving them treatment like some sort of psychological massage or physiotherapy for the mind, and yet nevertheless that they claim 'to enable the client to do what he could not do before'. This is not as absurd as it sounds. The objection arises from the difficulty of recognizing a method of helping (or enabling) that is radically different from methods by which one person acts on another with the minimum of personal and emotional involvement between them. Involvement here means more than co-operation. In counselling, the client is not passively co-operative like someone reclining in the dentist's chair, or having a physical examination. On the contrary, he is invited to co-operate actively in the discussion, which cannot make headway without his participation. He discusses issues that he feels strongly about, provided he is willing to discuss them. He is encouraged to do this but in no way compelled or urged to. His involvement in the interview is crucial since the two of them cannot put their heads together on his problem unless he is willing to explain what it is and how it affects him.

The distinction between these two groups of relationship (expert giving treatment to a patient or counsellor and client discussing as colleagues) is crucial to an understanding of counselling and to the successful use of the role. It is the task of the present chapter to clarify this difference.

Earlier it was suggested that counselling is a particular application of the principles of casework and that casework is a particular application of the principles of psychotherapy. We must now add a further dimension and say that psychotherapy is derived from psychoanalysis. This spectrum of depth, skill, training and function is of enormous range. At the one extreme is the analyst, the most skilled and specialized of all, whose training has extended over some eight years and involved a personal analysis as well as theoretical training and practical experience under detailed and continuous supervision. At the other end are the men and women for whom this book is written. They are alert to the personal and emotional needs of people who need their help, in whatever vocation they normally work. Counselling offers them a different way of helping from that which their usual role provides. This comparison is not intended to belittle the counsellor (compared with caseworker or psychotherapist) but to highlight the continuous strand of theory and practice running throughout these ways of working. There is a consistent base on which these helping activities rest and it distinguishes them from the authoritarian group of methods we have just considered. But before we go on to outline the essentials of a psychotherapeutic approach there are some further preliminaries to look at.

We must start by sorting out some of the terms, because there is a good deal of common confusion about them in ordinary conversation. This arises from the fact that the material of psychotherapy (its subject matter) is not a limited speciality of the practitioner as is the subject matter of other highly technical vocations, say spectrum analysis, microbiology or crystallography. On the contrary, it is of close personal concern to everybody since its material is the human personality and the way it functions in relation to others and to the conditions of contemporary society.

Perhaps the most popular view of the psychoanalyst or psychiatrist is that of the cartoonist. The bearded expert, pompously bespectacled, with his diploma hanging on the wall, and his patient (an ordinary person like you or me) reclining ominously on his couch, invites many a humorous caption, contrasting the absurdly pretentious, specialized approach of the expert on human nature with the common-sense of the common man. Jocular terms like 'head-shrinker', 'trick cyclist' and humorous definitions (such as 'one who keeps his wife under the bed because he thinks she is a little potty') tell the same tale. These are perhaps equivalent to the cartoons of bishops who slipped on banana skins in earlier days. Those who boast (or seem to boast) of being authorities on our common human destiny must expect to feel the force of our debunking, in the same way that we like to make jokes about computers. And it is not only in cartoons that the psychiatrist is a figure of fun. Which of us does not know someone who knows a psychiatrist who is madder than his patients?

It is important in the present context for the reader to clarify his personal orientation in relation to psychotherapy. This will help to avoid throwing the psychiatrist out with the bath-water or ignoring what we can learn from him because we lose patience with his (supposed) claims or his sometimes incomprehensible jargon. It is crucial to the helpful practice of counselling that the reader sorts out his own position in relation to the key concepts of psychotherapy.

First, however, we should distinguish between psychotherapy and psychiatry. A psychiatrist is, by definition, medically qualified. He has also qualified in the study and treatment of mental illness and abnormality, as other doctors may specialize in diseases of the ear, nose and throat, or some other branch of medicine. Like any other doctor, the psychiatrist may practise privately or in the Health Service, or sometimes both.

From a layman's (or a patient's) point of view, the psychiatrist is usually encountered at the out-patient clinic at the local hospital or at some special clinic as in child guidance. He is also found, of course, on the staff of a mental hospital or of the psychiatric department of a general hospital. A patient reaches a psychiatrist (like any other medical specialist) through the recommendation of his own general practitioner. The psychiatrist may treat him by any of various methods as he judges appropriate to his patient's condition, for instance by chemical means (prescribed drugs), by psychotherapy, by physical means such as electro-convulsive therapy, by medical or surgical treatment of any condition that is causing the patient's illness, or sometimes by a combination of approaches. The psychiatrist also takes note of environmental factors affecting the illness or recovery of his patient and may thus be concerned with the personal relationships or social conditions affecting him. These aspects he will often seek to ameliorate through a psychiatric social worker (a qualified social worker who has taken further training in mental health) who works as a member of the psychiatric team.

Psychotherapy is unfortunately not a precise term and it is not therefore legally limited. Anyone can, if he wishes, call himself a psychotherapist but he cannot call himself a psychiatrist unless he is medically qualified. Similarly anyone may call himself a counsellor. The difficulty is really one of definition. Fortunately, in the United Kingdom (with its National Health Service) there are fewer temptations for people marginally qualified or unqualified to set themselves up as psychotherapists or counsellors, and exploit members of the public. Although I do not know of any precedent, it seems probable that anyone paying for treatment by psychotherapy might have a legal remedy if the individual giving the treatment did so without training, though just what might satisfy a court as adequate training might be a matter of lengthy argument.

While, therefore, one can only define psychotherapists and counsellors as people who practise these two methods of helping, it is possible to narrow down a description of their methods and of the theoretical basis on which these rest. Indeed, we have already attempted this in the opening chapters, so far as counselling is concerned. Something must now be said about psychotherapy.

For our present purpose the general ideology and the usual pattern and atmosphere of a psychotherapeutic interview are not far different from those already outlined as characteristic of counselling. Both give a client or patient opportunities for recognizing ideas, values and attitudes that he had not fully realized he held. He may find, for instance, that he has some that are contradictory, and that he holds strong but opposite feelings towards a person, a topic, an issue, a memory or a fantasy. Both counsellor and therapist are listeners and colleagues with whom these discoveries can be shared, willing to discuss them and their implications in relation to whatever difficulty the client is facing. In this way the client begins to discover that at least some parts of his problems make a kind of sense when studied in the company of someone who is not concerned with passing judgment or siding with or against him, and who neither becomes a partisan nor rejects him with disapproval. This strengthens the client's recognition of how he is involved in the circumstances that surround him, which previously perhaps he mistook as totally external acts of a malignant fate or hostile people. He becomes freer then to choose what he will do and how he will manage his affairs, because previously his autonomy was limited by his own spontaneous and irrational reactions, which he had never understood and could not control.

This may seem a bold claim for counselling and certainly, expressed in this shortened way, it is so. But people do get a new slant on their problems and fresh encouragement and ability to deal with them from a discussion (or more usually a series of discussions) of a counselling nature.

The same is true to a greater degree in psychotherapy. The therapist (because of his extended training) is able to discern in a tentative way further complications and inconsistencies in his client's emotional attitudes towards important issues in his life. He is able, therefore, to take the client much farther into a reappraisal of his inner strength and weakness, his contradictory feelings, and the unrecognized parts of his own personality that limit his freedom and emotional stability in the conditions that he finds upsetting. These discoveries can be worrying and throw the client or patient off-balance emotionally so that he may for a while become emotionally dependent on the therapist, at other times disappointed in him or hostile to him, at still others afraid of him. At some stages his reactions towards the therapist are a puzzling combination of several of these attitudes, a Babel of conflicting feelings clamouring for expression and, as it were, shouting one another down. This is a difficult stage in the therapy for both of them. It is here that the therapist is distinguishable from the counsellor. The counsellor will tend to soft-pedal these situations to keep things within bounds. He will treat such storms

E

as interruptions in their reationship so far as it is aimed at a more realistic appraisal of the problems the client is facing and which the counselling aims to relieve. That is to say, the counsellor's work is directed towards an understanding and resolution of what the difficulty means to this particular client. He sees the problem as the reason for their discussion. What the client discovers about himself and his own attitudes and values, aims and desires, is important to the extent (and only to the extent) that it plays a part in the problem under discussion.

For the therapist this does not go far enough. For him the patient's response to the difficulties that beset him are characteristic of him, though in just what way may take a lot of unravelling. The psychotherapist's focus of attention is not on the problem and how the patient reacts to (or possibly causes) it, so much as on the patient himself, his contradictory attitudes and feelings and the way he relates to the therapist himself during their discussions and, indeed, between the sessions.

Because of his training, the therapist is better equipped to sense the areas of difficulty in the patient's life. He will hear more in the same words that the patient might have used to a counsellor. The counsellor prompts his client to say more about issues that seem important to the situation (that is, both the actual counselling and the predicament that the client is in), and so does the therapist. But the therapist will, so to speak, make better guesses as to the next stage of the process – the unravelling of obscure and unconscious emotional issues and the facing of their implications. In addition to his greater perceptiveness, he will be better equipped to withstand the pressure if his patient's emotions are directed towards him. He will appreciate their significance more fully than a counsellor is able to do, and with less spontaneous and possibly unhelpful reaction.

How is it that the therapist has these greater abilities? It is not simply that he has read more than the counsellor, has attended more lectures and seminars on the theory behind his vocation or has attended an academic course in psychotherapy. In fact, there is no such course since the practice of psychotherapy is a skill that depends only partly on abstract or academic knowledge. The essential feature of a psychotherapist's training is his own analysis. This is the means by which his perceptiveness is sharpened so that he can immediately apply his background of theory to the issue confronting him during treatment sessions with his patients. And it is also the means by which he is able to accept the emotional onslaughts of hostility or emotional dependence, the frustrations and hostility, the anxiety and confusion with which his patient greets the deeper understanding of his own reactions, the problems arising within his personality and symbolized either by the therapist himself or projected on to him. In essence, psychotherapy is a means by which underlying unconscious emotional factors within a personality may be brought to light and faced. Its importance as therapy in relieving emotional distress, and the compulsive reactions and uncontrolled impulses that are unhelpful to the patient's daily life and are factors in his internal unhappiness, is something that has to be experienced to be believed. This is unfortunately inherent in the methodology. Just as the patient cannot come to terms with unconscious areas of his personality without skilled help, so the would-be therapist cannot do this for himself except by the same means. He may have read all the works of the masters in psychoanalysis (though he would be old by the time he had done it), attended endless series of lectures on psychology, and still be as far as he was at the outset from being relieved of the burden of his own unconscious restrictions and irrational emotional reactions to situations that are stressful to himself. Not only this, but he will very likely have become more adept than he was originally at explaining himself to himself and thus rationalizing his own inner situation which remains as deeply concealed from his conscious appraisal as it was before.

There is something of a closed circle in this description to which critics of psychotherapy are accustomed to draw attention. There is an echo of the Taoist saying, 'Those who know don't speak. Those who speak don't know.' This gives to psychotherapy an elusive arrogance of inner conviction that is maddening to those who require a rational explanation of how it works, a convincing proof or at least an explanation. Moreover, it gives to psychotherapists an aura of exclusiveness, even clannishness, as though they are devotees of some mysterious cult that is only accessible after initiation rites (namely, the therapist's own analysis at the hands of another therapist). It is difficult to see how this impression of a priesthood, handed down by open doctrine but secret ritual, can be altogether avoided. The uninitiated who have an opportunity to hear (or overhear) psychotherapists and analysts discussing theoretical aspects of their work are likely to be more convinced than ever that they are not talking about human nature and personality but indulging in some esoteric mumbo-jumbo that is exclusively their own. Critics of analytical therapy are, moreover, not slow to indicate the apparent loftiness with which their objections may be met, namely the bland assertion that these criticisms are nothing but defences against the threat from the critics' own unconscious drives.

The reader will inevitably be concerned to find his own position in this ideological conflict. He may cherish his own convictions or prejudices, in favour or against the claims of psychotherapy to bring help of a unique kind to those whose internal emotional life is confused and unhappy. But he can scarcely dismiss the issue as unimportant. For it is demonstrably true that our emotions are not wholly within our control. This fact lies at the very heart of counselling as it does of psychotherapy. A moment's consideration of sexual impotence in a man (or sexual frigidity in a woman) will serve as an illustration. The rival claims of various forms of treatment for this distressing condition cannot disguise the self-evident fact that the difficulty is beyond the sufferer's conscious control. Indeed, the absurdity of urging him to try harder, to pull himself together, to exert himself and so forth are evidence that his disability is not rationally subject to his own control or indeed to the control of those who thus urge or criticize him. The powerlessness of the sufferer to help himself by taking thought is further proof. Most people can without difficulty recognize (in others if not in themselves) emotional reactions that they cannot control, and most of us are sometimes taken by surprise. We know that our feelings sometimes betray us. For instance, by shyness or blushing, an abhorrence of some harmless object, a topic that never fails to arouse our fury, guilt, shame or inquisitiveness, people who attract or repel us against our better judgment, a feeling of elation or dejection unrelated to events or even in defiance of them, a mood that we cannot control, a situation that arouses our anxiety although there is no recognizable threat, the grip that some tales, pictures, music unaccountably have upon us, situations that put us on the defensive or on the war-path without apparent reason, isolated acts that make us exclaim 'I don't know why I said (or did) that', the dreams we have at night or the day-dreams when we loosen our control of attention – all these are largely uncontrollable. They become the province of psychotherapy if they interfere with daily life or are distressing to the individual or those around him.

The therapist aims to bring a degree of order into this chaos. But it is not an order imposed by himself. He helps the search for meaning in these events, these emotions, so that the individual may increase the area of his freedom of choice and of his personal autonomy. To treat the symptom without involving the meaning it has for the individual sufferer may be justified in some circumstances, for instance when it has such serious consequences for himself or others that almost any attempt to divert the unconscious drive behind the symptom is worth attempting. But such methods as aversion therapy or hypnosis are not available to the counsellor and need not concern him so far as his own work is concerned. The same is true for the psychotherapist, with an important proviso. As a lay therapist working in a medical context he is more likely than a counsellor to meet patients who are psychologically ill. Since the therapist is treating a patient whose emotional condition may have a physical origin it is obviously incumbent on him to make sure that medical aspects have been professionally assessed and treated. His concern is with the psychological and emotional factors that are involved, not with the physical. And it is not within his competence to decide on the medical issue. The patient therefore is normally (in his own interest) referred to a lay psychotherapist only after first being seen by a psychiatrist, so that medical aspects have been fully assessed and, when necessary, attended to.

There are some who maintain that counselling (at any rate when extended over a series of interviews) should not be undertaken except with the knowledge of the client's general practitioner. Though, since counselling is concerned with personal, social environmental relationships and the client's response to problems arising in them, such a precaution may seem unnecessary. Nevertheless, in institutions where there is medical cover for the lay counsellor this is a valuable adjunct as, for instance, among those student-counsellors who are lucky enough

to be working as members of a student health service in which
it is simple for the counsellor or the client to be seen by a doctor.

Before leaving the counsellor's relation to psychotherapy we
should consider a further criticism. It is often objected that there
is little if any evidence that will stand up to scientific scrutiny
on which to base the assumption that psychotherapy is effective.
A great deal of professional controversy centres around this.
Sometimes, indeed, it is reminiscent of the theological and philosophical disputes of the schoolmen of former times who, to the
uninitiated, seem to take a peculiarly self-satisfied delight in
academic arguments and scholastic hair-splitting so robustly
mocked by Rabelais and Laurence Sterne – writers (one sometimes
feels) who should be living at this hour.

The problem seems to involve not merely a difference of
conceptual framework but incompatible criteria. It is as though
someone demands proof that a picture or a poem or a piece of
music is effective, that it 'works', that the time and care spent
on it are justified. The well-known joke about the time-and-
motion study of an orchestra playing a symphony is a similar
example. But so prone are we, laymen and professionals alike,
to revere the physical sciences that it is perhaps all too easy to
assume that only activities that can be proved effective by
criteria based on measurement can legitimately claim to be
effective. But just as no work of art can be proved effective by
measurement (since artistic criteria are not measurable) so it
may be argued that the joint task on which psychotherapist
and patient are engaged cannot be assessed by scientific method.
Indeed, it is difficult enough to define cure, sickness or health in
physical medicine and much more difficult in psychological or
emotional terms. One quickly gets bogged down in further
definition and in value judgments and distinctions of a socio-
logical, philosophical, ethical or religious nature. The one side
of this dispute seems to say to the other 'I cannot accept as
valid the claim that your work is effective unless I can satisfy
myself by my own criteria that it is so', to which the other in
effect replies, 'But your criteria are not valid to assess what my
work is about. To reject a claim to success or effectiveness because
it does not satisfy your *a priori* scale of judgment can hardly be
called scientific.' Meanwhile emotionally sick and unhappy
people have to get what help they can, wherever they can.

A further example of this dispute occurs in courts of law where psychiatrists are brought in as expert witnesses and sometimes exasperate the learned judge by the lack of legally satisfying clarity in their evidence. Both judge and witness are highly intelligent people but their frames of reference are so different that it sometimes seems scarcely possible for there to be any real communication between them. One might think that academic and research psychologists would come to the rescue in this stalemate and devise means of assessment acceptable to both the critics and the psychotherapists. Unfortunately, however, it is the psychologists themselves who seem to be the stumbling-block, since it is from them that the distrust of any but measurable criteria mainly emanates.

The counsellor, operating at a relatively superficial level and dealing only with values and issues that his client can consciously recognize (though sometimes with distress or difficulty) and discuss with him, has an easier task than the psychotherapist. The resolution of some relationship that has reached an impasse, the decision that has hitherto been impossible to make, the crisis that has been averted in a manner satisfying both to the client and to others around him, and to both his and their immediate and long-term interests, are evidence of the effectiveness of the counsellor's work without worrying too much whether or not he can prove the outcome is successful to the satisfaction of anyone but the client himself. If this is further evidence that the counsellor is really operating on a basis of faith (albeit a faith shared by his client) then that must be accepted. It seems at least no worse than accepting adverse judgments on his efforts made according to criteria that are not relevant. As a psychiatrist once told me, 'When a patient says to me "I am better", then I accept it'. It is only fair to add that many psychotherapists would not accept this evidence as valid since it might be an unconscious device by which the patient is safeguarding his deeper conflicts from the pain of discovery.

We must now consider a few common misunderstandings about psychotherapy among many educated people. One is the false assumption that the therapist is only (or at least primarily) concerned with the most unpleasant side of a patient's life, anything that by ordinary social standards would be considered disgusting, unacceptable, vicious, cruel, amoral, immoral or wicked. This is a half truth. In the process of therapy that is devoid of moral judgment, a patient is free to bring to the light of day aspects of himself that he cannot normally discuss with anyone. The belief that only neurotic patients or the mentally sick have such aspects of their personality is demonstrably incorrect since it is often precisely the most correct, upright, righteous, respectable people in whom such unwelcome traits are most prominent, once given the opportunity of expression. Such a discovery is of course painful and humiliating for them, as it is for anyone. But we keep (albeit unconsciously) such aspects of our personality buried beyond awareness to our own limiting. The more effectively we keep them at bay the more rigid we become, the more prone to intolerance, to being shocked at the frailties of other people, the more filled with righteous indignation at those who transgress the bounds of decency, morality or respectability, and the more compulsively we have to convince ourselves of our own cleanliness and uprightness. This is not insincerity on our part, but a weakness disguised as moral strength. Our resulting intolerance arises as a defence against the unacceptable part of ourselves.

The psychotherapist is not concerned primarily with whether his patient's drives, wishes, aims, fantasies are socially respectable or shameful. He is concerned with whatever exists. Therefore he does not (as he is sometimes accused of doing) delve around looking for all the psychological filth he can unearth. He tries to help his patient to see what in fact is there. Indeed, one outcome of psychotherapy (as of counselling) is the discovery not only of unacceptable sides to the patient or client, but of hitherto unrecognized and unaccepted traits of love and creativity that have never found adequate expression.

A further common mistrust of psychotherapy is the belief that to acknowledge the primitive, unacceptable, cruel or disgusting side of oneself is highly dangerous and bound to lead to its outward expression. This view, in my experience, is specially common among those who cannot accept the moral neutrality of our emotions because of the belief that wrong thoughts are themselves sinful or immoral. It arises also from a lack of trust in the ability of men and women to control their actions even when they cannot control their feelings, thoughts, fantasies and dreams.

SUMMARY

Internal and external aspects of difficulties – the counsellor not an authority, leader or idealist – therapy and equality of status – casework, psychotherapy, analysis – psychiatrist and psychiatric social worker – opposite feelings towards the therapist – psychotherapist focuses on the person rather than the problem – his training – unconscious factors – emotions not within conscious control – contrast with aversion therapy or hypnosis – difficulty in scientific evaluation of success – psychologists – misunderstandings about therapy – traits of love and creativity – moral neutrality of feelings.

CHAPTER 5

Casework and Relationship Therapy

Casework was bred by psychotherapy out of social work. The theory and practice of psychotherapy impregnated the body of social work, and casework sprang from the union. It would be tempting to take this analogy farther and consider the growth and development of casework from its infancy to its present maturity and ask ourselves what it inherited from both parents and what rivalries remain.

But that would lead us too far from the main purpose of this chapter, which is to clarify some of the practical and theoretical issues that confront the counsellor-reader. Many of these become clearer from considering casework. Before the momentous union, social work constituted a conscious, rational attempt to close the gap between environmental conditions and individual adjustment. Early pioneers of social work (to their lasting credit) had brought a humane concern for human suffering and handicap to practical expression through relief of poverty and the improvement of social conditions.

These elements of the social work tradition still exist. There are individuals and organizations today devoted to improving the lot of people who live in conditions of Dickensian squalor, cruelty or neglect, in the face of which the refinements of counselling, casework or psychotherapy seem irrelevant luxuries. Neither the welfare state nor casework therapy has displaced the dual need for both the practical improvement of social conditions and personal help by which individuals may become more competent at improving their own life and happiness and their relationships to others. It is all the more regrettable when rivalries spring up between those who claim that nothing except improving social conditions has any lasting effect and those who claim that nothing but the skilled treatment of individual maladjustment will ultimately improve a client's condition.

We are here concerned with effectiveness. To bring comfort and relief to the unhappy, the handicapped, the incompetent is an undeniable moral good and if casework or psychological theory leads anyone to think otherwise so much the worse for them. Equally, it is an undeniable moral good to improve social conditions so that poverty, handicap and incompetence are diminished and their impact lessened. Both approaches help to diminish the total of personal suffering. One works collectively, the other with individuals.

Counselling, casework and psychotherapy are also methods that diminish suffering, though not just by relieving and comforting individuals nor by improving environmental conditions. Whether it is better to rehouse or subsidize a 'socially inadequate' family, relieve them by material help or treat the psychological and personal springs of their inadequacy and so develop their competence, are not exclusive alternatives. It is to the credit of present-day social workers that they make use of any of these three different approaches. However, it is sometimes unpractical or ineffective for the one worker to fulfil more than one role. This is a familiar issue during in-service tutorial discussions with caseworkers or counsellors. Under the pressure and stress of a heavy load of work, it is tempting to try to settle such doubts once and for all by a rigid definition of role. But this oversimplifies the issue, for the choice depends on many factors. In practice, the urgency of the issue usually determines which comes first – environmental adjustment, practical relief or personal counselling. The urgency of choosing the appropriate course is not always inherent in the problem, as it appears to be. It may be in the worker, whose anxieties are aroused by some issue that is of critical (and usually unconscious) concern to himself. He cannot sort this out alone but may be helped to do so in a case discussion group.

Social workers tend to fall into two ideological parties. In the one are those who maintain that social conditions are the predetermining factor behind social maladjustment, whether this is labelled inadequacy, delinquency, incompetence or anything else. Thus (they argue) it is futile to devote one's energies to the more sophisticated aspects of casework, concentrating on the life-history and former experiences or even on today's psychological stresses in personal relationships, instead of seeking first to ameliorate the present social conditions in which the client or his family live and work. Therefore (they maintain) we should collectively highlight the effects of adverse social conditions on those victims who live in them, and should bring pressure to bear on local or national authorities to remedy such conditions. These arguments may be supported by social theory or observations of animal behaviour, by social psychology, anthropology, ethology and Marxism and its derivatives. Character, behaviour and personal happiness are, according to this view, determined primarily (if not wholly) by the pressure of external conditions on the individual. 'We are' (claim this group), 'social workers not psychotherapists.'

The other group refute such arguments by pointing out the general nature of the observations and deductions on which their rivals rely, and the erroneous assumption that bad social conditions invariably cause social inadequacy. In the view of this second group, this is an obvious fallacy since they can quote examples where different clients have reacted in totally different ways to the same set of external, social conditions. Indeed (they claim) in some instances clients have unconsciously caused the conditions or at least have gravitated towards them, just as people who assume that others are always hostile to them will bring this about by unconscious means and then say 'There you are'. This second group argue that generalizations (even when based on large samples of the population) may be valid in predicting trends or probabilities but tell one nothing at all about any individual. Thus (they go on) to regard social conditions as the cause of individual social problems is misleading and in the end self-defeating. Although some change in conditions may be warranted on the grounds of relieving unhappiness or suffering, the only effective way to treat the individual is by an examination of what these external conditions mean to him, how he reacts to them, whether or not he in some way needs or seeks or causes them or whether he can alter them or remove himself from them. Conditions are significant only for the impact they make on individuals (they say) and to assume that they affect all people in the same way is demonstrably incorrect.

These two factions within the casework professions summarize their differences by claiming, on the one hand, 'Basically, we are social workers not psychotherapists' or, on the contrary, 'Basically we are dealing with the human nature of individuals, each of whom has a different temperament, a different life-experience, a different scale of values and aims, both conscious and unconscious. Therefore, whether we like it or not, we are dealing with the psychology of the individual.'

This dilemma arises again and again in the experience of individual caseworkers, as it does in conferences and in in-service training groups. One often hears social workers (voluntary and professional) say 'We are not psychologists. As social workers we must deal with social conditions.' Sometimes they fiercely resist the individual, personal approach as though it were dangerous, unethical or obscene.

Those social workers who are more in sympathy with individual clients than with the generalized, collective or external aspects of their work explain that difficulties which disturb a client (or a whole family) often turn out to be presenting problems, a cry for help, a symptom. These are social problems only when viewed collectively. Seen through the eyes of the individual client they represent merely the idiom in which he is expressing some internal, personal, emotional or psychological difficulty or maladjustment. This view sometimes exasperates those who see such problems as socially determined, and they are seldom convinced by illustrations from experience or the case histories of others.

It is tempting to attribute these two views to the contrasting temperaments of the caseworkers. The extroverted look naturally to externals for explanations of personal behaviour and attitude. The introverts look inwards at subjective and individual factors. But one can attribute the same differences to age, tradition or training. In most casework professions there are 'the old guard' who quote the way they were trained, their experience and successes, the literature on which their approach is based. Sometimes they will fight with determination to resist the incursion or obtrusion of what they regard as new-fangled psychological theories, far-fetched and extravagant or fanciful explanations of quite simple external observable facts, like overcrowding or illiteracy. Metaphorically they disprove (to their own satisfaction at least) the subjectivist theories of the others, like Dr Johnson kicking a stone and thus disproving the arguments of the idealists. Unfortunately this argument never convinces their opponents who maintain that it is no more than an irrelevant defence against the psychological threat of subjectivism.

A similar dispute arises in more sophisticated form in some of the rival schools of psychotherapy, where varying emphasis is placed on the importance of social and family influences in the moulding of personality. American writers generally tend more towards the extroverted, external, socially-determined view of personal development than their European counterparts.

The same dichotomy arises sometimes in discussions about the personal, pastoral work of clergy, among marriage counsellors, and in the approach of individual interviewers in Citizens' Advice Bureaux, some of whom exclaim 'We are not caseworkers' as ardently as their counterparts claim 'We are not psycho-therapists'. (And some of the latter may sometimes be heard exclaiming 'We are not analysts'.)

The relevance of these somewhat unedifying disputes to the practical work of the counsellor-reader is this. These arguments arise when some particular issue is under discussion. The rest of the time the work goes on without such professional rivalries. Most counsellors, social workers and caseworkers operate between both limits, the external and the internal. They are concerned with some external, environmental condition or limiting frame-work and also with its impact and meaning for the individual client who is in difficulty. Some workers no doubt tend to the one or the other view of their work and of their client's needs, partly through their own temperament or personality-type, partly from the way they were trained, partly from the prevailing ideo-logy of the group within which they are working and partly, perhaps, from some new shift in professional expertise, some change of direction in their vocational pendulum, some over-throw of established technique.

The same point can be illustrated by tape-recorded interviews. The trainee successfully follows his client's train of thought and tries to throw new light on its implications for the difficulty he is in, sometimes clarifying a point, sometimes merely showing his continuing interest, sometimes making a link with something the client described earlier. While this process continues, factual questions about conditions and external details scarcely enter into the discussion. But when suddenly the caseworker feels stuck, becomes self-conscious, loses the train of his client's thought and feeling he is apt to intervene with a factual question. This sequence of events happens so often (as can easily be discovered by anyone who cares to try the experiment) that it must surely have a meaning. A sudden switch to a factual, extroverted question invites attention to what was happening between the two participants immediately before it. If the tape is turned back and the caseworker and a tutor (or experienced colleague) listen carefully to what has been discussed they can usually find the explanation, especially if they listen not merely to the literal meaning of the words but to the feelings conveyed by tone of voice and manner of speaking. Sometimes, in ordinary conversation, we switch from an emotionally-charged topic quite deliberately, to save ourselves or the other person from embarrassment or pain. We all know what it is to change the subject, as we say, to get away from the thin ice of guilt or shame, anger or sorrow by a deft diversion on to some unemotional factual, external detail, some piece of information or recapitulation, or a a new topic. We do this when we notice that the other shows signs of distress or when we feel anxiety or embarrassment arising within ourselves, whether or not we realize what occasions it. When we do know, we steer clear of the painful or upsetting subject. When we do not know, we remain vulnerable to further surprise attacks of unease.

It seems probable that a professionalized version of this process happens when counsellors or caseworkers suddenly feel constrained to protest that they 'are not psychotherapists' in order to justify shifting their attention from a disturbing or worrying aspect of the discussion to the safe ground of factual information or extroverted and environmental concern. If this is indeed correct (as I believe it to be) then it goes some way to explaining the passion with which some workers defend their practical, circumstantial approach to the problems that confront them and their sometimes intemperate scorn for colleagues who (sometimes with equal scorn) criticize them for concentrating on the surface or outward expression of what is really inwardly difficult for the client.

Most groups of counsellors or caseworkers contain at least one member who is the spontaneous spokesman for the anxieties of the rest. A discussion of the inward, introverted issues of a parti-cularly difficult or worrying case provokes such a spokesman to a sudden outburst that it is all becoming too far-fetched, too deep, too theoretical, too psychological. This is usually followed by an appeal to reason, to come down to earth, an assertion that it is all really quite simple, that it resembles a similar case in which the speaker applied common-sense with immediately successful results, and that this proves all this delving to be a waste of time.

Such an outburst challenges other members of the group to discover for themselves where they stand, both in the particular instance being discussed and in their general approach to the work. It illustrates a common tendency to seek safety from the pressure of internal issues by moving into the external. Generalizing is another example of the same manœuvre. For example, any new group of caseworkers need time to be able to trust one another with the emotional, personal aspects of their work. Preliminary discussions therefore start on safe ground, sometimes dealing with the externals of a case, more often with some generalized issue. A group of student-counsellors, for instance, will start with someone asking about student grants and parental contributions or whether students should receive loans rather than grants. Even when a group has been working together for several months, any member may introduce a worry-ing case evasively. Have the others, he asks, read some particular book on (for instance) drug addiction? He may then make reference to one part of the book, dealing perhaps with the relative harmlessness of smoking pot. He may quote other opinions, for instance that the habit leads to experimenting with hard drugs, or something of the kind. Such generalized dis-cussion soon becomes desultory and no one is much interested. Perhaps one of the members (or the person leading the group) will ask the original speaker whether he had any particular instance in mind. He will then, if the previous discussion has reassured him, come out with the details of what is worrying him.

This roundabout approach is so common that it is a normal feature of this type of work. So it is of counselling. Any counsellor, no matter what context he works in, becomes familiar with the client who begins in just the same fashion, asking only a generalized, safe question as it were to test the ice before he can bring himself to what is troubling him. Many clients begin with what is often termed the 'presenting problem'. If reassured by the counsellor's attitude and the atmosphere of the interview, he may be brave enough to explain what is deeply worrying him. Sometimes counsellors are tempted to regard the presenting problem as of little importance, except as an introductory gambit. But often it is of real importance to the client and indeed may be urgent and critical. A student nurse, perhaps, has made an appointment to give in her notice, as it is the last day of the month. At this final moment she wonders if it is the right decision. Or a husband on the verge of divorce proceedings must decide today whether to turn back or go ahead. Anyone, like the student nurse, may have decided to throw his hand in, to leave the university or technical college, to leave home, to leave anything, to resign or start on something new and at the very last moment a host of anxieties assail him as to the implications and consequences. Such urgent worries are far from trivial even though they are symbols of deeper difficulties.

In these instances, familiar to any counsellor, one recognizes again the duality of the relatively safe, external, impersonal aspects of the discussion and, behind these, the more deeply worrying, internal, personal aspects, of which the former may be the presenting problem or external manifestation of some inner crisis of indecision.

A vivid example of this duality (that may sometimes seem a dilemma) occurs regularly in the work of the Citizens' Advice Bureaux, that infallible source of information on any conceivable subject which may be had, literally, for the asking. Sometimes it is difficult to know just what the enquirer is seeking. 'How can I find accommodation?' may be a simple and emotionally uncomplicated request for information made by someone who has newly moved into the district. Or it may be a desperate cry from the heart of a wife who has walked – or flounced – out of her marriage, or an alcoholic who has been thrown out by an irate landlady, or an adolescent rebelling against his parents. 'How does one get a divorce?' may be an emotionless, factual question asked by someone on behalf of a friend, or it may be a sabre-rattling threat from a husband or wife at the very limit of their tolerance and with matrimonial murder in their heart.

F

'How can I trace a sailor?' may be merely a frivolous wish to send him a valentine or the alarm of a girl who is pregnant, cannot face the outraged fury of her family and is desperately considering abortion or suicide.

Those who deal daily with such inquiries ask themselves what is their function. Are they counsellors or are they never more than information-givers? What exactly does Advice mean in their title? While perhaps most of the inquiries that come to them are straightforward requests for information, some unmistakably are not. They are only marginal to the inquirer's concern, sometimes not so much a presenting problem as the only available way to get a hearing on some worrying difficulty.

It is thus inevitable that in C.A.B. training courses one should hear the dilemma, 'Are we there to give simple information or to act as counsellors?' Some say with conviction 'We are not counsellors' just as counsellors exclaim in self-defence 'We are not caseworkers' (and so on). But the fact remains that any interviewer is a person, a fellow human-being who will from time to time be challenged to relieve suffering or help with troubles of a personal and emotional kind, to find or indicate some way out of a situation that has become intolerable or that has inherent in it much personal distress, anxiety or frustration. Even if 'we are not counsellors', which of us can with an easy conscience dismiss such cries for help as lying outside our role? We may avoid this quandary by claiming we are not sufficiently trained to be caseworkers but then our conscience makes us ask just how is one trained to be a fellow human-being? Or we desperately try to think of someone else better equipped to deal with this problem and we direct the problem to them but uneasily suspect we have rejected the person with it. There are good reasons for keeping casework and associated activities on a professional footing. But can we keep humanity on a professional footing or be content to decline such personal help as we could give on the grounds that it is outside our terms of reference or beyond our competence? Can there really be a demarcation line between professionalism and humanity? If indeed there is, then we are back again (or may at any moment be) at what I have criticized as the white-coat syndrome of the professional non-counsellor. This question of acceptance or rejection of the personal aspects of work with people has to be faced whenever it arises. Under the guise of 'involvement' (or of transference and counter-transference) it is never far from any concern with personal help, or indeed any professional help for people. A further discussion of this issue must wait for a later chapter.

All this is familiar enough in casework literature and training, where involvement is disparaged as unprofessional. What is less easily recognized is that the counsellor (and, indeed, those who train him – or write books for him) perpetually face the same choice. Will he deal with the external or the internal aspects of the problem that confronts him or the training he is giving? It is not enough to recognize that some people who seek help nevertheless try to evade their basic worry and substitute practical, factual concerns. It is much more important (and much more difficult) to notice how the counsellor himself does this. In training establishments, the institution itself exemplifies the anxiety to keep on safe ground. One person cannot help another to come to the deeply-felt personal issues of what concerns him without entering into a truly personal, committed relationship with him. Therefore to teach casework, counselling or psychotherapy in the context of an academic institution is extremely difficult. First, there is the barrier provided by the institution and second, the barrier made by an academic environment. The segregation of staff and students, necessary as it may be for institutional reasons, makes any personal relationship between individuals or between teacher and small group seem out of place and may render it so unconventional as to seem subversive. How is it possible to reconcile such a structure with the ideology of counselling? Any institution is a collective, sometimes a combination of several collectives, and therefore liable to irrationality and impersonality. This atmosphere is incompatible with the personal and individual training required for counselling, however necessary it may be for other purposes. Is it not likely that the disquiet about this situation, about being treated impersonally at the very stage of development where one is most concerned to establish personal, individual identity, is a factor behind student unrest? At least it may seem so, since the older universities, with their personal tutorial system playing a more prominent part in the student's life, have been on the whole less subject to irrational and collective revolt.

No counsellor can ever be too wary of the natural tendency to evade personal issues in the ways we have been considering. Unhappily, it is easier to recognize it in others than in oneself. It is always wise, if one can, to become increasingly alert to one's own use of such devices, the tendency to theorize, to generalize, to rely on formality, facts, convention, practical aspects as defences against the pressure of personal, emotional involvement. This recognition is crucial if we are to develop the skill required in counselling. But it is something which cannot be done effectively by oneself. Something can be achieved by self-observation and reflection, but not much. Therefore any counsellor (or professional person acting from time to time in a counselling role) is handicapped if he has to work in isolation from any supportive or training contact with other people doing similar work. Hence the value of small regular groups for in-service training through case discussion.

These aspects of counselling may be summed up as a retreat from the personal to the impersonal. As in military bulletins, we may perhaps avoid so strong a term as retreat and speak of strategic withdrawal (nearly always to higher ground). This is a useful phrase here because it is precisely what is happening. A counsellor or a client withdraws from personal involvement for strategic reasons. But the strategy is usually unconscious and spontaneous. Nevertheless, the shift on to higher and safer ground means the choice of ground that suits oneself – and that is strategy.

But another factor is recognizable. If the two parties unconsciously agree to make this withdrawal (because the topic or the relationship is becoming too personal) and leave matters on that safe ground, the heat and liveliness fade out of the discussion. This happens in training-groups as in counselling interviews. It can be observed in tape recordings which become palpably dull or even boring both to listener and to the participants when the discussion gets stuck on safe ground. There are two contradictory issues behind this. One is a person's need for recognition of what concerns him deeply, personally, emotionally. The other is a feeling of anxiety, even panic, at the danger of revealing himself to another person, for fear of rejection. In practice, most counselling interviews and discussions waver between these two. Both counsellor and client tend to start on safe ground, then find this is not what they want to discuss, then approach nearer to the personal, internal worries or frustrations involved in it, then shy away again on to some technicality, practicality or factual detail, get bored with that and try again. This constant wavering is not undesirable or a waste of time. Such strategic withdrawals are, indeed, essential. But the counsellor needs, if possible, to be a little bolder than his client and sense when is the time to bring the discussion back to more personal concerns. This is a crucial part of the counsellor's skill but it cannot be developed merely by taking thought, only by trial and error. Sometimes a counsellor goes too slowly, leaving the discussion on safe ground for so long that the client loses interest. At other times the counsellor may too brusquely keep the topic on sensitive, even painful ground only to find that his client can outmanœuvre him by some new and unexpected withdrawal. At other times, less easily recognized unfortunately, the client raises questions that are too difficult, too personal, too anxious for the counsellor. Then it is he who makes the strategic retreat, for instance by reverting to facts. 'How old did you say you are?'

A theoretical approach to counselling, casework or psychotherapy is perhaps one of the most insidious defences by which any counsellor may keep himself permanently on safe ground. It is very difficult to convince intelligent counsellors that their intelligence is not an important part of their job. It plays a small part but it is much less important than their perceptiveness, their inner emotional stability and flexibility. Indeed, anyone who trains counsellors has to resist the traditional tendency to adopt an intellectual approach to training. It is no more than marginally and initially helpful. Over and over again, small training groups fall back on abstract and intellectual concepts to explain events that puzzle them and, indeed, to explain (or explain away) emotional conflicts and difficulties. One such device (another strategic withdrawal) is the use of technical terms, as though by labelling a person or a situation we have somehow helped to overcome it. In a similar way an intelligent counsellor may become persistently concerned with explanatory or descriptive systems borrowed from sociology or psychology and thereby hide from himself the unacceptable fact that problems in the personal life are not resolved by explanation alone.

It sometimes takes counsellors a long time and much meta-phorical sweat and tears to get past this barrier, and unfortunately it is very difficult indeed for a writer to be much help with it, simply because a two-way relationship between reader and author is impossible. Lecturing is little better, and even a small tutorial group will be ineffective if tutor and trainees uncon-sciously conspire to avoid personal involvement and treat their project at an intellectual level only, not by feeling but only by talking about feeling. This is the same pitfall as was described in a previous chapter that leads a counsellor into a position of intellectual or psychological superiority (not holier but more insightful than thou). That is a denial of the possibility of a mutual involvement in the client's problem, as being too hurtful for him or too threatening for the counsellor.

The social worker's choice of working at an environmental or at a personal level (discussed in Chapter 4) illustrates this same point. The either/or quality of discussions about casework (or about the work of the Citizens' Advice Bureaux or any other counselling service) illustrates the same anxiety about the internal and personal factors of such work. That common question 'How far should we go?' (or sometimes 'How deep should we go?') is not simply a request for a ruling on the precise demarcation line between, say, information-giving and counselling, counselling and casework, or casework and psychotherapy. It is also the generalized expression of personal anxiety arising from the stress of a case that the questioner has in hand or an inner anxiety about his ability to help his clients constructively with their emotional problems. Or it may be a combination of both these.

In casework, however, the worker boldly embraces both shadowy horns of this apparent dilemma. He is actively concerned with environmental, social factors and also with their emotional significance to his client and to himself. This dual concern is the specific contribution that casework can make to professional help for troubled people in the complex problems and situations that confront them. Caseworkers who complain that they sometimes find themselves in a role with authoritarian overtones or over-tones of a giving or withholding character that interfere with their proper function are, I believe, expressing a stress that is inherent in their work. This is where discussion with colleagues can be so helpful, because it can enable the individual to find what is best in all the circumstances of the situation confronting him – the potentialities of a counselling role or of environmental change, of authority or therapy, of providing or not providing some material help at that juncture and for that particular client. Such important considerations would be by-passed by a rigid ruling on whether we are or are not therapists. An all-or-nothing approach is a simple but sterile way of brushing under the carpet the various types of issue that confront a caseworker. Sometimes he will envy the more specialized role of others; the psychotherapist (unconcerned with environmental factors except as a framework within which his patient leads his life) or those who just give what information they are asked for or concern themselves only with environmental change without being challenged by the emotional concerns and conflicts of their clients.

However, the caseworker's sometimes unenviable lot of operating within two frames of reference that are sometimes incompatible is really the strength of his contribution. For his client is also involved in the same kind of predicament, the personal and the impersonal parts of his life. The caseworker lives daily with the task of somehow reconciling these two aspects of every case he handles. Therefore he has to face daily the conflict within himself, whether to work in any one case (indeed in any interview) on the personal or the impersonal level, without wholly excluding either. Some caseworkers tend more in the one direction than the other, just as all of us, counsellors and clients alike, tend more towards introversion or extroversion in every department of our lives and in all our relationships.

Neither the external nor the internal factors can be eliminated without unreality (that is to say, the unreality of busying oneself with externals to the neglect of the personality of the client or, on the contrary, neglecting important practical matters because of an exclusive concern with the psychological). Therefore the caseworker more easily recognizes that he is primarily dealing with relationships. The irritation or anxiety behind demands for a final and dogmatic answer to what our role is arise from the difficulty of reconciling incompatibles. Sometimes these incompatibles are a husband and wife, or an employer and employed, a young person and an authority figure, a club member and the club itself or the leader, a student and his parents or tutor – all these are relationships, as is the clash between environmental conditions and the individual person. Most of us faced with such incompatibles tend to take sides, because reconciliation is the most difficult task of all. If we can deny the existence of one side of a relationship we are freed from the burden involved in recognizing the importance of both. But by doing this we deny the potentiality of the relationship and render ourselves impotent to help.

Cumbersome as it is, the expression Relationship Therapy expresses the common ground between counselling, casework and psychotherapy. It is the groundwork of reconciliation, the method by which incompatibles can be helped to change from sterile or destructive disharmony to creative harmony. The term reconciliation may suggest a mere erasure of differences, a denial of opposites or some process by which they may be masked or suppressed. But a relationship built on such a basis would be fragile and inharmonious because of unconscious resentment at having to surrender to the demands of another person without actively accepting the differences underlying the incompatibility. To be accurately described as therapy, the task of the counsellor cannot depend on such one-sided suppression or even on a two-sided agreement to suppress differences, as anyone knows who has mistaken an agreement to compromise for the ability to compromise.

Critics of psychotherapy sometimes accuse its practitioners of reducing the personality to a colourless and docile neutrality in face of the controversies of daily life. This mistake arises from supposing that our own hotly-defended arguments, convictions or prejudices are somehow an essential part of our identity without which we would be mere ciphers. In reality, any release from the unconscious limitations on our adaptability results not in conformity or neutrality of a negative kind but in the release of new possibilities of creativity, untrammelled by restrictions of an aggressive-defensive nature that unconsciously keep us perpetually on the defensive or the attack. Perhaps this is too bold a claim for the relationship therapy that is possible for most counsellors but it is at least the direction in which their healing ministry aims, a restoration of wholeness not of biological function but of personality and its relationships, of which the psychosomatic expression is one aspect.

SUMMARY

Origin of social work – improvement of conditions and personal help – presenting problems – rival schools – use of taped interviews – switching from feelings to facts – safe ground in an interview – clients who test the ice – duality of internal and external aspects – professionalism and humanity – involvement, transference – difficulty of teaching counselling in an academic institution – withdrawal from personal involvement – unconscious agreement to withdraw – contradictory issues – theoretical approach can be a defence – intellectual concepts and technical terms – explanatory or descriptive systems – pitfalls for training – personal anxiety – reconciliation, a difficult task – direction of counsellor's healing ministry.

CHAPTER 6

The Scope of Personal Counselling

At the beginning of Chapter 1 counselling was described as a dialogue in which one person helps another who has some difficulty that is important to him. We went on to consider some of the implications of personal rather than impersonal counselling. Any issue that is important to someone must be to that extent personal, in the sense that its significance is specific to him. His difficulty arouses his feelings. It has some kind of value for him personally, and he reacts to it emotionally. His reaction may be hostile or friendly, passive or active, helpful or unhelpful, desirable or undesirable, good or bad. The focus of the counselling is the way his difficulty affects him, not what it might mean to others (including the counsellor).

The reason for adopting this approach is that personal difficulties arise not merely from external, objective events but from the nature of the feelings that these events arouse in the person who faces them. Any adviser has encountered people who are unable to accept the most sensible or expert advice, are unable to follow a course of action that they agree is desirable, necessary or even essential to their own interests or their well-being. No amount of persuasion or explanation is effective in overcoming their inability to do what they admit is right, proper or desirable, even though they want to do it.

This situation is understandably exasperating to the busy professional adviser or the harassed friend, relative or well-wisher. Often people can accept the advice they are given and can act on it. At other times they cannot accept it, however soundly based it is. At yet others, they do accept it, but are unable to act on it. In the first of these three instances no counselling is called for, because there is no personal difficulty. The advice is accepted even though it may be unpalatable (for instance, if it involves an operation or making economies or moving house). The unpleasant feelings associated with it are tolerated not only because the soundness of the advice is recognized. There are no overriding, internal (and probably unconscious) emotional barriers.

But the inability to accept sound, expert advice (or if accepted, to act on it) creates a baffling situation. The professional adviser, in the best interests of his client or patient, does his best to persuade him to do what is advised. If he still refuses, what then? The adviser may point out the probable consequences of his refusal. He may suggest calling in another expert, on the assumption that the refusal rests on mistrust of his own judgment. Or he may explain the situation to a friend or close relative and try to enlist his help in overcoming the reluctance. Or he may fall back on whatever powers of persuasion he may have. Finally, if all these fail, he may have to wash his hands of the situation and explain that he cannot be held responsible for the consequences. Personal counselling, as outlined in these chapters, provides him with an alternative way of approach. It is not quite so paradoxical as it may appear, namely that it persuades people by not trying to persuade them. This is a half truth. Counselling can enable the client to choose either of the two alternatives confronting him, or sometimes to find other alternatives. It is a process of enabling a person to do what he could not do before. It does not determine what he should do or impose any solution on him. It provides a way of resolving the stalemate ('I know that's right but I can't do it') or the dilemma ('There are only two alternatives and I can't do either').

Why is it that some people can accept sensible or expert advice and others cannot? Or why is it that the same person can accept it on some occasions or in some contexts but not in others? The answer does not lie in their erroneous thinking, because that can be put right by explanation. It lies in their inner feelings. Fears, anxieties, anger, frustration can sometimes be alleviated by explanation and then the initial reluctance may be overcome and agreement reached. But sometimes this is not possible. Anyone knows, for instance, the folly of trying to overcome another person's conviction or prejudice, anxiety or anger by rational argument. People may be made to comply outwardly by intimidation, by authority, threat or promise, by cajolery or trickery or by playing on their suggestibility. But they cannot become free to choose by these methods which are in any case manipulative and unethical.

Fortunately for professional advisers (and anyone else whose work involves dealing with people) most of us, most of the time, *can* accept the sensible thing to do, *can* see reason and accept authoritative advice and some measure of authoritarian control. That is to say, most of us most of the time are reasonable beings and adequately law-abiding. But it must also be said that there are circumstances in which we are not reasonable or law-abiding and, in fact, are (at least momentarily) quite unable to be so. We say we were provoked or tempted or were foolish or acted without thought or lost control or saw red or got the jitters, or we say that for some inexplicable reason we were not ourselves, acted on the spur of the moment and out of character, sometimes adding we cannot think what made us do it. As we get older we grow more adept at avoiding situations in which we act outside our normal character-ideal. We learn to control ourselves and change the subject or do something else when we feel the familiar alarm-bell. But sometimes we are caught unawares.

Most people pride themselves on their rationality and may be perfectly justified in doing so. Lesser beings adopt a kind of benevolent and indulgent tolerance of these irrational chinks in their armour of rectitude, goodness and kindness. Professionally we tend to surround ourselves with traditional safeguards of formality so as to lessen the likelihood of being surprised by our own irrational sensibilities.

This latter safeguard can greatly inhibit counselling since formality and rigidity or professional or vocational rituals or roles make it difficult to establish the relaxed, personal, open atmosphere of the counselling interview. It is the white-coat syndrome again. Similarly, it may be very difficult for a client to shed his own role-costume and be himself. People who daily fulfil a professional role of any kind have many advantages in situations where they decide to help through counselling rather than their normal expertise. But shedding the familiar uniform is a necessary and sometimes difficult preliminary. Indeed, this is often a major contribution of in-service training and I have sometimes been tempted to suggest we put 'Cloakroom' on the door of the room where such a group meets!

Counselling is concerned with people's feelings, and it acts through their feelings. This is because the difficulties that we refer to as personal (meaning individual to ourselves) are intractable precisely to the degree that they are based on feelings we do not fully understand and therefore cannot fully control by rationality. This is as true for the counsellor as for the client he is trying to help. He is able to help partly because of his training and partly because he is not involved in precisely the same predicament as his client. His own feelings may indeed lead his rational judgment astray or at least warp or distort it, but since he is not concerned with trying to provide any particular solution, this need not unduly handicap him. Of course, the counsellor may be subject to unconscious internal and emotional pressures of his own that are aroused by the personality or the predicament of his client and this will limit the extent to which he can help him. But this is a more complicated situation that we must consider later, under the heading of involvement.

The client who seeks or is offered help from a counsellor may realize part of the emotional significance that his difficulty has for him. He knows that he cannot face an examination or an operation or a divorce or a legal action or his father or his boss, because he is afraid. But this may be only half the truth. He may know that he is frightened but not why he is afraid or what it is he is actually afraid of. Superficially he does know. He will say that anyone in his shoes would feel the same. This may indeed be so. It may be a frightening situation, where perhaps it would be more peculiar if he were not afraid than that he is. But he may still not realize the exact nature of the threat. This is important because fear, like other emotions, affects us more severely when we do not understand its origin. Indeed, the fears, furies and frustrations that beset us are far less rational and far less conscious than we usually suppose. This is easier to see in others than in oneself. We may appreciate why someone should be afraid or angry or frustrated, but are sometimes at a loss to understand the degree of their emotion, its intractability, their inability to cope with it, to lead their lives in spite of it, to lay it aside sufficiently to come to a decision sensibly and on good advice, to act rationally even though they are deeply involved emotionally. We may sympathize with but not understand them. 'I do see how you feel but I don't understand why you feel it so strongly.' If we say this we may get the reply 'Neither do I' or perhaps 'If you were *me* you would'.

It is often difficult to realize how little our deepest and strongest feelings can be controlled rationally. That is why counselling is almost impossible for people whose personality is basically authoritarian. They are at a loss when a client's feelings will not change and are apt to lose patience at what they regard as his obstinacy in not changing them. What possible answer can such a person give to the common admission 'I know I shouldn't feel that way, but I do' or 'I know it shouldn't affect me that way, but it does' or 'I know I should love my husband (or wife or child or parent) but I don't'? Counselling is a way of elucidating those aspects of personality that are vitally important to a person's happiness, efficiency and well-being but are not directly and fully within his conscious control.

This is particularly true of personal relationships. Indeed, the whole of counselling is concerned with relationships in a wide sense. That is to say, concerned not only with the way people get along with others at home, at work, at leisure but also with their relationship to external conditions, to changes in their environment and even, in a subtle sense, in the relationship between different aspects of themselves. This latter is not so far-fetched as may at first appear. When we say 'I was not myself' or 'I lost control of myself' or 'That is not the real me' we acknowledge that somehow we can feel split, not so much into different parts as different aspects. I may contrast what I would like to be and what I have to admit I am, or what I am and what people take me for. This is why counselling, casework and psychotherapy are all aspects of relationship therapy. Each is concerned with estrangement and reconciliation, with restoring a working harmony between differences, so that what seemed to be incompatible may become complementary, whether these are conflicting issues, conflicting individuals or conflicting aspects of the client himself. The word therapy may justifiably be used in this non-medical sense because counselling is directed towards the establishment of a dynamic wholeness, a satisfying and creative integration that is characteristic of emotional, psychological and social health.

There is a parallel between a patient consulting his doctor and a client consulting a counsellor (whether voluntarily or on someone else's initiative). The commonest reason (though not the only one) that takes any of us to a doctor is pain or discomfort and our aim is to get relief. Similarly, a client's primary aim in counselling is usually the alleviation of distress. To both doctor and counsellor, however, the pain or distress are not the only aspect. In the long run they may not be the most important. Pain and distress are in a sense by-products or symptoms of dysfunction, a sign that something is wrong, though not an immediate indication of *what* is wrong.

A counsellor, however, is not solely concerned to bring to light the emotional significance of the client's predicament, so that he can cope with it rationally, make a sensible decision or act on advice that he knows to be sound. These are common and important aspects of counselling, but its scope is wider.

The distress caused by an inharmonious relationship can be crippling, particularly when the feelings it arouses are largely unconscious in origin. Indeed, is it too much to say the commonest (though not perhaps the greatest) source of happiness or unhappiness lies in the quality of our personal relationships? Many years of counselling have convinced me that this is true for very many people, though perhaps those for whom it is not true would be unlikely to consult a counsellor. They would be unlikely to recognize the existence of personal difficulties of an internal, emotional kind, let alone seek help with them. A bank manager, a doctor, a solicitor or a priest might find in their experience that other factors are more significant.

Some of those who consult counsellors are well aware that their immediate problem is but a crisis in some personal relationship, a culmination of an increasing estrangement or an explosion of incompatible emotional drives, a clash of personalities, an outburst of rivalry or hostility, a rebellion against the constriction of some too-possessive relationship or a desperate bid for love or loyalty that is being denied.

Frequently an exploration of the precipitating crisis brings to light a situation of emotional conflict in which the client is unable to make any adjustment in his relationship because he is torn within himself by opposing aims, incompatible drives, opposite feelings or unattainable objectives. The problem that finally brings him to the counsellor (or challenges the counsellor to intervene and offer his help) is fraught with so much unhappiness and personal distress, such urgency or desperation that it may dominate the foreground and make any concern with what led up to it seem irrelevant or evasive. Yet there is always a background, because no one stumbles into an emotional crisis that is completely unparalleled in his own experience. The outer circumstances may be totally new to him but their inner, emotional significance scarcely can be. Indeed, the very experiences that are most painful, most unforeseen, most unnerving are those that reactivate emotional experiences that have occurred before. They left us vulnerable because in some way we were unable either to assimilate them or deal with them to our own satisfaction. Later chapters in this book will attempt to make this assertion clearer, but any counsellor can test it for himself. Provided the client is not too much shocked emotionally by the problem that brings him to the counsellor, he will usually find little difficulty in recollecting, with the counsellor's help, other experiences that have affected him in a similar way.

Unfortunately this may lead either of them to the conclusion that the initial experience (which is simply the earliest that the client remembers) must be the cause of the others. This is a common misunderstanding of dynamic psychology. In reality the link between an earlier, unhappy emotional experience and the client's present distress is much more complicated than simple cause and effect. Nevertheless, for most people (and perhaps for all) there are certain combinations of circumstances, of an extremely complex kind, that may fortuitously be repeated and issue in some intense distress or difficult crisis. From the counsellor's point of view (that is, for the purpose of helping his client) it is useful to explore such difficulties in the present or the past or as foreseen for the future. The time sequence is not important since the link is not causal in any important sense. The usefulness of such discussion lies in the increasing ability of counsellor and client to discover what are the main factors that constitute the client's difficulties.

What is likely to emerge is that there are certain types of situation to which he is particularly vulnerable, that upset him, that make him so angry or so anxious, so frightened or so frustrated that he cannot cope with the demands made upon him in a realistic way that satisfies himself and others. Counselling can at least help to bring to light the type of difficulty that upsets him in such a way and to such a degree.

This is a constructive and encouraging experience though initially it may seem to the client (or even to the counsellor) to be merely highlighting what he cannot do rather than finding what he can. Or it may seem to ignore the immediate crisis and waste time looking for similar experiences in the past. But these two aspects are not incompatible. Trying to see a client's difficulty more clearly does not mean one ignores the pressing and practical issues that confront him in today's problem. On the contrary, it enables both client and counsellor to get a more realistic view of what the difficulty is and what is required if it is to be dealt with satisfactorily. Those who are used to working on a basis of problems and solutions may easily slip into adopting a similar approach to the personal relationship difficulties that are the province of the counsellor. They may then propose some solution that the client is unable to accept or unable to put into effect. Once again, we are back at the question of ability not solution, of helping people not solving problems.

Most counsellors are prone to overestimate a client's ability to manage his relationships in a more satisfactory way, to feel differently, to control his feelings more rationally. Indeed, whether counsellors or not, do we not all tend to hold other people more responsible for their feelings than we ourselves are for ours? It is so easy to assume that because other people would behave differently if they felt differently, therefore they can feel differently if only they will make the effort. The truth is, all of us are emotionally vulnerable to events and to people in ways that we do not fully recognize. We tend to find causes outside ourselves or at least outside our control, so far as we ourselves are concerned. But for others we tend to have a different yardstick and believe they reacted as they did, on purpose. In practice, the interplay between oneself and outside events or other people is immensely complex. Fortunately we do not need to bother much about it most of the time. But when some important difficulty arises in one's personal life, then we do need to understand more fully what is happening.

The importance of unconscious factors in limiting or determining the way we react to events and to people is paramount.

G

This is the source of the irrationality of our emotional reactions and our limited ability to control or re-direct them. The task of exploring these factors is highly skilled, immensely pains-taking and makes great emotional demands on the therapist. Such work is primarily the province of the psychotherapist or analyst. But nothing is achieved by regarding unconscious factors in personal life as some mysterious forbidden territory, since it is an essential aspect of humanity and of personality. A counsellor is wise to steer a middle course (if he can) between trying to adopt psychotherapeutic techniques out of some text-book and, as it were, dabbling in the interpretation of unconscious phenomena (which will be futile and may be risky to himself and those he aims to help) or, at the other extreme, turning away as though with a shudder from the pervading influence of unconscious factors and attempting to help his clients under-stand their difficulties better and find more effective ways of dealing with them by purely rational means.

This dilemma is central to the counsellor's role and its resolu-tion is necessary for the helpful practice of his vocation. It is a personal dilemma for any counsellor, both in the sense of being individual to himself and in the sense of its internal emotional significance. The counsellor faces an interplay between external events and environmental conditions on the one hand and internal, emotional reactions and conflicts on the other. He also inevitably faces the interplay between conscious and uncon-scious factors in the clients he tries to help, in himself during his work and in the way he approaches it. The way he copes with this dilemma affects the relationships he makes with his clients collectively and individually.

For these reasons earlier chapters of this book have considered the relationship between counselling, casework and psychotherapy in general terms. I believe it is unrealistic to make precise demarcation lines and, for example, maintain that only the psychotherapist should trespass into the area of unconscious motivation or involvement. These aspects of personality inevit-ably enter into any relationship whether social, professional, marital, vocational or any other. It cannot be hoped that if you ignore them they will go away, and it would be quite unrealistic to maintain that we can leave unconscious phenomena to the psychotherapist and help people emotionally through reason and common-sense alone. It is important, therefore, in any book on counselling to try to make clear where the individual counsellor will place himself in respect to the emotional and unconscious factors that are always present in personal problems and difficulties (including his own). It would, however, be equally unrealistic to insist that any counsellor should have had a personal analysis before trying to help people by counselling. This is unpractical for two reasons. The first is the time and expense involved. The second is the unwillingness of most normal people to undertake any such training, even if the time and money are available.

In previous chapters we have considered the relation between the various divisions of relationship therapy. These are convenient but necessarily indefinite and variable. Any counsellor, caseworker or psychotherapist may from time to time work in ways that are characteristic of one of the other ways than his normal one, and he may be fully justified in doing this. What matters is that his choice should be realistic in terms of his own ability and training, and the requirements of the situation he is handling and the person he is helping. One of the main aims of this book is to help him to make these choices, not once and for all but throughout his experience in personal counselling.

It is sometimes claimed that there are more precise demarcation lines between these approaches than I am suggesting. Some say that the basis of psychotherapy is that a doctor (or non-medical trained analyst) treats a sick patient, whereas the counsellor is helping a normal person in distress. This is, in my view, an unhelpful half-truth. How does one define sickness when referring to an individual's personal, emotional involvement in the problems and difficulties of his personal life? It is of course true that mentally sick people may come the way of the counsellor, or any other adviser, and that counselling may not be an adequate way to help them. But a non-medical counsellor cannot be expected to make a psychiatric diagnosis, though he can be helped to recognize the presence of factors that make his kind of help ineffective.

A more important objection to this somewhat glib distinction is that psychotherapy and counselling can often help even very sick people. Moreover, there are individuals whose personality is so rigidly defended that they deny the existence of any internal emotional difficulties, which they compulsively and unconsciously project on to others. Superficially such people may seem thoroughly competent and successful but to the psychotherapist they are (at least potentially) sick. However, his distinction between health and sickness would be very different from that of a doctor or social worker who has no sympathy with an analytical approach to human nature and its difficulties.

We shall have to consider this question again when we come to deal with psychological health and sickness in Chapter 10. For the present we should return to the individual counsellor-reader's choice of how he will work in any particular instance. Since there are many options open to him, it is necessary to consider his relationship with his individual clients, since this distinguishes counselling from other kinds of interviewing. We shall not repeat what was said in earlier chapters. There we were concerned to distinguish counselling in general from other forms of interviewing. We are now concerned with the relationship between the two individuals who meet to discuss a difficulty. The following are some characteristics of this relationship.

First, lack of pressure from the counsellor. It is helpful if the counsellor is not pressed for time. If he is, his attention will be divided and he will be likely to miss important but subtle implications in what his client tells him. Pressure of time may work on the counsellor in a different way from clock-watching, however. His own anxiety arising from within the relationship or from external factors may tend to make him hurry and press the client to come to the point more quickly. It is therefore better to deal with his own anxieties in other ways, independently of the interview, if he can. If the counsellor is unhurried it will greatly help the client to fumble around for those aspects of his difficulties that are not readily available to him for description. And these are often the most important aspects of them.

The counsellor's ability to resist the urge to do something, take some action on behalf of the client or regard the situation purely in practical, extroverted, active terms may at first perplex his worried client. But it will help him to come round to the feelings that are aroused by his difficulties or are giving rise to them.

A client is helped to look at his situation broadly to the extent that the counsellor resists the temptation to bring authoritative pressure on to him either by giving expert advice, or by trying to persuade him in some direction or by implying some moral judgment.

The relative absence of these pressures reassures worried, frightened or angry people and allows them to expand their thoughts and feelings. Conversely, of course, they will be restricted by these or any other pressures put upon them during the discussion.

Second, acceptance of a valid difficulty. If a counsellor recognizes the validity of his client's problem he will be in a better position to explore it with him and discover some of the less obvious factors involved in it. This is not simply to sympathize with him, to know that one would feel as he does if one were in his place. More important than this is an understanding that is partly intellectual and partly emotional. One can grasp what the situation is only through what the client is able to communicate and what the counsellor is able to receive. The counsellor grasps the literal meaning of what is being described to him. Through his perceptiveness he will also grasp at least part of what emotional factors enter into it both at the present interview and in what has preceded it and brought the two of them together. This dual understanding is not exclusive to relationship therapy. It occurs in any personal relationship where one troubled person is lucky enough to be able to discuss his problem with someone who recognizes it as valid through this dual understanding of head and heart. It is more or less what is meant when we say 'Go and see so-and-so about it. I'm sure he will understand.'

This may be contrasted with the response of those who do not, in this dual sense, understand because they are unable to grasp the validity of the impact which the situation is making on the individual. Anyone who is ready to listen will grasp the facts. What is crucial is the perceptive empathy by which he senses the predicament of the other person. If he does not, then he is likely to feel baffled or impatient, to think the other is making an exaggerated fuss, harping on some quite ordinary little complication, or is just crazy or incomprehensible. Such uncomprehending reactions are unfortunately common. They arise, perhaps, not from any lack of compassion but from an inability to sense what is involved, or a failure to recognize the reality of the difficulty in terms of this individual and his particular circumstances. No one is helped by those who say (or imply) 'But I don't see what all the fuss is about' or 'But why should that upset you so?' or 'But it's perfectly simple really, you don't need to get so worked up'. These responses betray a lack of perceptiveness. The speaker may be warm-hearted and kindly-disposed, but he is just unable to grasp the emotional significance of the other's predicament. This ability can be trained and it is an important ingredient in counselling.

Third, clarification of meaning for the client, not the counsellor. A sensitive understanding of what the client has outlined is a useful start. It is still more helpful when followed by a shared discussion in which both participants begin to see it all more clearly, begin to recognize and discuss the various factors contributing to the problem, whether these are external and environmental, internal and emotional or an interaction between both. This encourages the client because he begins to see daylight in his confused situation or his intractable conflict or dilemma. This is all the more helpful because it has come from discussion, from a shared exploration and is not handed to him on a plate by the expert to take or leave. He is himself involved in the increasing clarification and begins to see that his difficulty makes sense, and that it is a kind of sense that can be shared with another person and understood more fully with his co-operation.

Fourth, a recognition of the validity of feeling. If the counsellor can accept both the client's problem and his feelings as equally real and (in his circumstances) valid, it will help him both to grasp and to tolerate the part they play in the difficulty. Strong feelings are not usually acceptable in ordinary social relationships. They are apt to cause embarrassment and make people unwelcome as friends, companions, colleagues. Therefore most social relationships involve some degree of unreality. We need to keep the expression of our strongest feelings under some control. In a counselling interview a client is under no such restraint. In contrast to the habit of having to conceal his strongest feelings, he will find himself encouraged to share them. The counsellor's tolerance of such expression is not to be had just for the asking. He too will have his own convention, his own limits of what he can tolerate from his client. But the more readily he can recognize that strong and unacceptable feelings are valid because they exist, and are probably important just because they cannot normally be expressed freely, then the greater will be the help he can offer and the freer his client will become. Indeed, most clients take fresh heart when they find that the counsellor tolerates the expression of what they feel inwardly but have been unable to express, and that he recognizes how valid are our strongest feelings and how little we can expect to clarify our difficulties without taking them into account.

Fifth, a tolerance of conflict. If both client and counsellor have been able to develop their discussion relatively free from constraint, then it is likely that contradictory elements will enter into it. People often have strong and opposite feelings about issues or people that are important to them (including those who interview them). This too is not normally acceptable. In ordinary daily life we are likely to find ourselves criticized for not knowing our own mind. It does not comply with common-sense that we should both love and hate the same person, both want and not want to achieve or possess something, both like and dislike our work or a colleague, both want to leave home and remain in it, both want and not want to take the lead or shoulder responsibility. We may also have conflicting or opposite motives behind many of our activities and ambitions. In a counselling interview (unlike a social or casual conversation) such conflicts are respected as significant just because they are often relevant to our inability to come to a decision or act effectively. This is why we dither, lose confidence and are pulled first one way and then the opposite. Conflicts and dilemmas are seldom resolved by considering the two alternatives (or opposite feelings) in more and more detail. What helps is to discover what is at stake. A free discussion may enable a client to recognize mixed feelings which he had not appreciated. Or he may come to realize there is a hidden aspect of his conflict. In ordinary social life one meets people who seem, for instance, over-anxious to persuade us of their like or dislike of an issue or an individual so that we begin to wonder whether they are trying to convince us or themselves. Is this, perhaps, because they are unable to recognize that they also have the opposite feeling? Such discoveries are common in a counselling interview. But it is not always easy or comfortable for the counsellor or for the client. People are often unable (not simply unwilling) to recognize feelings that are painful, shameful, worrying or unacceptable, threatening or confused. It may be a shock to discover their existence. Then it is easy to assume that if all the protests of loving have been found to be only one aspect of the situation, which also contains elements of hatred, then only the latter can be genuine. In fact, both may be genuine for our strongest feelings are seldom unmixed.

Sixth, personal acceptance. People in personal difficulties are not at their best. Inevitably they become self-centred, often intolerant, exaggerate their feelings or conceal them, become angry or helpless, self-pitying or demanding, impatient, resentful, childish or arrogant and suspicious, hostile or evasive. The counsellor cannot at first know the meaning of these attributes or see how they arise or what they indicate. But if he has understood the impact that personal difficulties, dilemmas and conflicts make on anyone, he will be able to accept these reactions as natural and inevitable. Socially, we do not do this. We usually dislike or avoid people who behave in these ways towards us. They can spoil a party, a meal, a conversation, a social gathering. Therefore in the interview it is probable that a client will try to control or hide his feelings. As he gains confidence from the relationship to the counsellor, he may suddenly give vent to pent-up feelings. This may startle or offend the counsellor if for the moment he has forgotten the object of the interview. This is not to conform to social convention and be pleasant but to come to grips with whatever is important and baffling to the individual client confronting him. Any client wants to show his best rather than his worst side, in counselling as anywhere else. But in the interview the one is no more and no less important than the other. This neutrality and acceptance (combined with a sustained attempt to find out what is difficult for him) greatly encourages a client. We are so used to being praised and accepted for what we can do well, liked for our good qualities, criticized for what is not acceptable, that it is often startlingly reassuring to find that one is not rejected or dismissed, scorned or criticized for showing reactions or voicing opinions that are socially unacceptable.

These, then, are six characteristics of most interviews in personal counselling. They are offered here not as standards to aim at

but in order to clarify the difference between this type of interview and others with which the reader may be more familiar.

SUMMARY

Clients may accept advice and act on it – or accept it but be unable to act
on it – or may be unable to do either – unconscious barriers – counselling
an alternative to persuasion – enables client to do what he could not do –
rational argument does not overcome prejudice – formality a safeguard
against surprise – unconscious pressures on the counsellor – counselling
impossible by those who are basically authoritarian – relationships to
others, to conditions, to aspects of oneself – relationship therapy, estrangement and reconciliation – therapy directed towards dynamic wholeness –
inharmonious relationships can be crippling – unattainable objectives –
reactivation of earlier experiences – clients vulnerable to certain situations – importance of unconscious factors – relation between conscious
and unconscious factors – projection of emotional difficulties – characteristics of the counselling relationship – lack of pressure – acceptance of
valid difficulty – clarification – validity of feeling – tolerance of conflict
and of opposite feelings – personal acceptance of people who are not at
their best and of socially unacceptable feelings.

PART II

CHAPTER 7

Dynamics of Relationship

In previous chapters we have been mainly concerned to see what personal counselling is, what contribution it can make to the happiness and effectiveness of personal relationships and what connection it has with other ways of helping. We must now consider how counselling works. What happens between counsellor and client during their discussions together? What enables the client to deal better with his personal problems and to improve his relationships?

The initial stage (as was mentioned earlier) resembles the common experience of discussing a personal difficulty with any good listener. This simple, unassuming experience is also the first step in counselling. But counselling does not stop there. It only warrants a particular name because it is distinguishable from the comforting but limited help that an untrained, unselected, unprofessional 'good listener' can give. Counselling, as we have said earlier, is concerned with relationships and with change. Sympathetic listening is often a recurring phase throughout any interview and may form a part of later discussions. It is not done once and for all at the beginning, though it *is* the beginning. Some new aspect of a difficulty may arise at any time in the discussions and then the client needs to talk freely, to express his feelings so that he can see them more clearly. In expressing them he has a chance to assess them, with the counsellor's help. A wife who bursts out in an interview 'Why won't you tell me what to do, that's your job, isn't it?' comes nearer to recognizing her hidden frustration than one who says calmly 'My husband won't make up his mind about anything'. The first is in a context that can be grasped (so to speak) while it is still hot. The second has by now cooled off and cannot be immediately grasped. It is an experience from the past for the client and secondhand for the counsellor, for whom it has been transposed into the present discussion.

This crucial point in counselling often remains a mystery for trainees and students. This is partly because a description may carry intellectual conviction but not really make emotional sense. This is the equivalent of the contrast just made. A trainee may say 'I don't really understand what the author means by a client *working-through* his problem.' This is all (so to speak) rather clean, clinical and remote. But if he spontaneously blurts out his unacceptance, or makes some ribald debunking caricature, or expresses his vehement disagreement and then finds that his comment is accepted and discussed, he will be helped towards a fuller and deeper understanding of how he has been challenged. and that (roughly) is what working-through means. A description could only be theoretical and could only satisfy him theoretically.

By experiencing and discussing his own reaction while he still feels it he can begin to understand what the issue means to him. This is seldom pleasant for him. He may feel he has made a fool of himself and fear he will be rejected or scorned for his explosion. He may believe that strong feelings are permissible in clients but not in counsellors. He may think he must not make value-judgments, as though any relationship could possibly be free of them. The tutor, in his turn, may be keen to help the students bring out their reactions to issues that arise in training but find difficulty in doing so because he too thinks strong feelings are disreputable or alarming. The tutor, conducting a seminar, would be in a parallel situation to the counsellor during an interview when the good listener phase merges into facing some challenging issue. If it all becomes too difficult he can withdraw and give lectures or write a book instead !

Being a good listener is more difficult than it sounds. A counsellor is, as it were, professionally committed to it if he can do it. But can he?

A client outlining a problem or difficulty may need help and encouragement. A good listener gives these and the client responds and is better able to express what he thinks and how he feels. But what he says and thinks and feels may not be acceptable to the counsellor, in the sense that it may embarrass, annoy or alarm him. The counsellor may try to hide these reactions but they probably show through. They may become too much for him and he is then unable to continue listening – so he interrupts and begins to ask questions, or comments on what has been said, or he mentions some marginal implication or possible solution to the external part of the difficulty. Counsellors cannot be universally loving or accept everything and everybody equally. Perhaps they would not be so helpful if they could. It would be daunting to be interviewed by a saint and one might feel 'How can he possibly understand what I am grappling with? He has got beyond all this.' That is how some of us may feel, now and then, towards a psychotherapist or analyst. But he does not rest content with our canonization and then we fit him out with horns and a tail. This sort of thing goes on in counselling, too, but less dramatically because the counsellor operates at a more conscious level and is more recognizably fallible. This is a useful safeguard. All the time he is sharing. Even when he can see more deeply into something his client tells him, he offers his thought for discussion. If it is dismissed or ignored he will leave it. He can afford to do so because if it is important to the client it will probably crop up again and eventually become discussible. The counsellor is unwise to hazard speculative interpretations of unconscious feeling in his client. If he does so he will change the basis of the co-operative relationship for the worse. Counsellors sometimes claim to be mirrors to their clients. I think this is an unhelpful role and possibly a little arrogant. It is more helpful, and more realistic, for the counsellor to realize he too makes mistakes and is not all wise or remote and unimplicated. He cares about his client and offers to look at his problems with him, to see how to make sense of them so that the client can then do something about them. People are helped by other people, not by reflections from a mirror. Admittedly it is the client's difficulties and personality that are the main subject of the discussion, not the counsellor's, but the relationship is mutual.

The listening stages of any interview involve both parties, though in different ways. Beneath the superficial meaning of what is described lie not only the inner feelings of them both but a gradual evolution of mutual acceptability. Either may be aware that he likes or dislikes the other, approves or disapproves of him, admires or looks down on him. The client is the one with the difficulty and therefore he is the first to test out the other and see what he can accept. The counsellor knows that acceptance is, in a sense, a condition of his helping. He therefore does his best to be accepting, no matter what his own inner feelings may be about this client or what he is saying. Sometimes it is quite clear how far a client is, as it were, daring the counsellor to reject him, or trying metaphorically to seduce him into taking sides, or taking up the cudgels on his behalf. It makes anyone anxious, to be confronted by another person and trying to describe what concerns us most. Shall we still be acceptable when we have shown more of ourselves or only if we continue to show ourselves at our best?

This anxiety arises whenever we share a deeply felt personal concern with somebody else, whether professionally or not. A mirror would frighten us. We wonder how the other person is going to react to what we tell them, that is to say, how they are going to react to us, to what we are. Hence we first bring out some relatively objective issue (as a 'presenting problem') to test the reaction.

Throughout most interviews there will recur exchanges in which the client is again testing the counsellor, noticing the reception he gets and responding accordingly. Counsellors also respond in their own way to what they are told, though it is difficult for them to recognize this.

The way counsellor and client react to each other gives both of them a chance to understand a little more deeply the client's scale of values in the relationships that matter to him. For the purposes of counselling (that is to say, in relation to the problem or difficulty about which someone is seeking help) it is useful to discover the limits of what can be accepted or tolerated, the conditions in which he can function best and most happily, and the kind of relationships that are easy or difficult, rewarding or restricting, for him. This is often of critical significance in what the difficulty means to the client. It therefore helps him to understand how to circumvent, overcome or evade this problem, or how he can come to accept it as limiting but manageable. This thaws out his hitherto insoluble dilemma or conflict, his irreconcilable or incompatible relationship. It helps him to regain a greater degree of personal freedom in adjusting his life to what he cannot change or finding new ways to deal with his old besetting problem.

The client's difficulty and how he can cope with it remain

central to the discussions. Other relationships, other issues, are relevant insofar as they impinge on this. Thus the relationship between client and counsellor, important as it is, is not the principal focus of their discussions. Its significance can be of real value in understanding what the client can or cannot do or tolerate. In psychotherapy, where deeply unconscious feelings and relationships are being explored, the nature of the relationship between patient and therapist *is* the central issue. The patient reacts more strongly and sometimes in ways that he feels are completely out of character. From time to time he becomes anxious, hostile and dependent towards the therapist, pleased and encouraged at the progress he is making, or depressed and defeated at the lack of it, seeing the therapist sometimes as a benevolent, kindly, supportive, comforting figure, sometimes as threatening or punitive. This kaleidoscope of feeling is deeper, less rational and more marked in psychotherapy than in counselling because the focus of attention is directed on to unconscious factors in the relationship rather than their relevance to the client's acknowledged problems and difficulties. In psychotherapy unconscious factors are traced to their source. In counselling they are not.

The reader who is familiar with the literature of casework or psychotherapy will recognize these reactions as transference. That is to say, the process by which a patient reacts to the therapist emotionally by associating him with important emotional relationships in his previous experience and of which he is now largely unconscious. This is not a simple process by which the patient is reminded of some person in his past – a parent perhaps, or other person who was important to him – it is spontaneous, automatic and outside his conscious understanding or control. He sometimes develops intense feelings of love or hatred, dependence, hostility or rivalry towards the therapist through unconsciously transferring on to him powerful feelings left over from some earlier relationship and reactivated in the therapy.

Although the counsellor has not been trained to work as a psychotherapist (that is to say, to concern himself with the meaning of deeply unconscious aspects of his client's personality) it is inevitable that he too will be subject to the same process, whether he is aware of this or not. Feelings will be transferred on to him in the same unconscious way. Moreover, this transfer

H

of unconscious feeling will colour the way he sees his individual clients. He will, for instance, meet some who inexplicably appeal to him, or arouse his resentment, or towards whom he feels protective or threatened, attracted or repulsed or on the defensive. This is not only a hazard of counselling. It occurs in daily life with all of us. It would probably not be totally eliminated from our experience even after a personal analysis, though it would be very greatly lessened.

The mutual reactions between counsellor and client play a decisive part in their relationship, because of these hidden factors. Few counsellors have either the confidence or the perceptiveness to bring them into the light of consciousness in a way that is helpful to their joint task. Indeed, this is perhaps the greatest pitfall awaiting any counsellor who makes a theoretical study of psychotherapy without the training that will help him to cope with his own unconscious and compulsive reactions to those he is trying to help. Most counsellors are aware of these dangers and defend themselves from them by not entering into too close, too theoretical or too speculative a relationship with their clients. A few sometimes become over-ambitious and then find it difficult to extricate themselves from the resulting entanglement in feelings of love or hate, dependence or rejection. Still others seek to avoid such risks by limiting the discussion to practical, rational topics and ignoring the emotionally-charged aspects of the client's difficulty. Much depends on the attitude and practice of the counsellor in the way he deals with spontaneous feelings aroused in his client and in himself by the matters they discuss. To avoid these topics would be to render counselling ineffectual. To wade out too far into deeply emotional waters and overestimate one's own ability to withstand emotional pressure from people in need of help is to risk an unhelpful entanglement. The best safeguard is to keep the actual problem or difficulty firmly in view and to explore or clarify feelings not for their own sake but in relation to the matters which bother the client.

Provided the counsellor maintains his role of co-operative partner in trying to make sense of his client's difficulties it is unlikely that he will either evade emotional issues or become unhelpfully entangled in them. The relationship between him and his client will change and vary as their discussions continue just as other close personal relationships change. For the counsellor, it is important to recognize this and to share his observations with his client. To grasp the significance of his client's reactions is not the same as enabling his client to grasp it, therefore explanation is seldom enough. It is all too easy to see causal links where none exist, and to offer explanations that a client may accept intellectually but without emotional conviction. Then he may feel that something important to him has been explained away. This can develop into a kind of game of applying concepts of psychology or psychotherapy and so rationalizing the situation that confronts them both. Pin-pointing a cause does little to help an individual cope with what is troubling him. It is always more helpful to ask a client to explain what any particular issue or event or person means to him than to hand him an explanation. It may be correct, but the purpose of the interview is to help the client find it out and deal with it. He will find new ways of dealing with his difficulties when he begins (with the counsellor's help) to see more clearly what they mean to him.

The counsellor can consciously aim to maintain this relationship of co-operation, of trying jointly to find how it is that his client cannot cope with some of his relationships yet can cope with others. He may need to resist his client's attempts to push him into some other role, to get him to become the benevolent authority or advocate or make him into a hostile figure. He will be less likely to get caught up in reacting compulsively against these unconscious pressures if he has realized how changeable his client's feelings towards him are likely to be.

These same issues arise in normal social relationships in which there are recognized stereotypes of behaviour, mannerism and feeling. It would be difficult to say exactly what is acceptable and what is not, though in practice we quickly discover. At a committee meeting for instance some apparently cold, innocent topic suddenly becomes emotionally charged. In spite of all the formality (designed, in part at least, to keep feelings under control so that decisions can, if possible, be made rationally) strong feelings sometimes burst through the businesslike calm. Someone speaks up with unmistakable tension in his voice, expresses himself controversially, his voice trembling as he strives to keep his feelings under control while he attacks or defends some possibility, opinion, decision 'on principle', or 'as a matter of principle'.

Sometimes, too, at a supper party something may touch off some explosive topic betwen two or more of the diners. Convention may momentarily fly with the wind and a heated argument begins. The tension may smoulder behind attempts to regain goodwill and conviviality, or it may continue throughout the evening or far into the night. Arguments are always a sign of irrational feelings which are not immediately obvious. Appeals to logic and reason are generally made by someone who holds most strongly some rigid attitude or point of view that is beyond discussion, let alone reason.

At other times, equally unexpectedly, a discussion that begins as a friendly social exchange may develop a depth of understanding that no one foresaw, in which some at least of those present are able to share topics, opinions, feelings that are dear to them but which they are not compelled to defend rigidly or others to attack.

These homely examples illustrate how the feeling side of our personalities is always (as it were) waiting in the wings for its cue, never predictable, always a source of uncertainty or interest, anxiety, anger or relief when it comes on stage, the prima donna from our unconscious.

Most normal people, most of the time, think they are fully aware of their own feelings, their own opinions, able to control them and subject them at any time to reason. We all pride ourselves on our reasonableness. But really it is seldom quite like this. Even in superficial, brief, conventional, social contacts we are from time to time aware of undercurrents of feeling, surprise attacks and defences, evasions, half-truths, double-meanings, subtle nuances of feeling or implication that are not easily explicable or expected. There are well-known topics on which half-hidden feelings and attitudes may be projected, for instance politics, religion, sex, social status, education – all familiar areas of controversy. There are also personalities who seem, as it were, equally controversial. Some people are argumentative apparently by nature, others make anyone else so. All the subtleties that enrich or bedevil relationships in a personal, emotional way, arise from a complex interplay of feeling, much of it irrational and partly or wholly unconscious.

This is the material of the novelist or playwright because it is the idiom in which he largely works, the interplay of feeling between his characters. We praise the creative writer for his imagination but perhaps this is not quite the faculty on which he most relies. He may have, as it were, some sixth sense by which he can hear and see and feel something more than you or I can. This perhaps provides him with a source from which he can assemble new combinations of relationship and into which he can spontaneously project aspects of himself. There is always an element of mystery in this or any other expression of creativity. I mention it here for two reasons. First, it is a factor that may unexpectedly enter into counselling when the counsellor witnesses with amazement some quite unforeseen constructive or creative advance by his client. Secondly, it is an illustration of the richness of that mysterious area in which our unconscious or half-conscious relationships have their being, the province not of science but of the literary arts.

The client who consults a counsellor (no matter on whose initiative) inevitably brings his past with him. The counsellor may know quite a lot about him but still not know him, though they may have met frequently in another context. Here, in the counselling, is an opportunity to get to know the person who seeks or is in need of help. This is not the same as knowing about him. It involves forming a relationship with him, and establishing a way of working together jointly. The counsellor does not know how this person has developed into the person he is now. Getting to know him will involve at least some understanding of where he has come in order to be where he is now, his development, his progress towards maturity, his ability to order his life satisfactorily and to cope with its stresses.

It is not enough for the counsellor to get to know him better. Sometimes the case histories in textbooks may give the reader this impression. Case histories are always written by the counsellor (or by another counsellor) or caseworker, not by the client himself. Why? He is not a party to this account. He is described as he revealed himself to the counsellor who does not know, perhaps, how *he* revealed himself to the client. This may lead a reader to believe that counselling does not involve himself personally, or should not involve him or need not. But this is a pipe-dream. Relationship therapy is not possible with a one-sided relationship. No one person can understand a relationship fully. No amount of training can make one an infallible or completely objective spectator.

A counsellor not only needs to listen and observe. He needs to know how to listen and what to listen for. It would be an interesting experiment to have six counsellors listen to the monologue of one client and then to ask each to write or record what he had heard. In earlier chapters I have suggested that a counsellor need not be particularly interested in assembling facts about his client. Instead he will be interested in getting to know him, so that he can discuss with him what is happening in his life, what are his stumbling blocks, his strength and weakness, and the alternatives that are or could be open to him, once he knows more clearly what the predicament means to him.

No precise scheme can be laid down for the new counsellor to follow. This would rid the discussion of its spontaneity and he would be led into using an impersonal questionnaire – a useful procedure for getting information one may want for some other purpose, but useless to help anyone learn more about himself and his unrecognized attitudes and feelings.

Trainee counsellors sometimes suggest that the secret lies in knowing what questions to ask, what promptings to give. In one sense this is true. The counsellor who knows how to listen and what to listen for will sense when and how to encourage his client to say more, to develop his line of thought or, on the contrary, he will sense when the interview has run up a cul-de-sac and will know how to find some new start.

But one cannot know the right questions in advance. Sometimes a counsellor who is unsure of his client (or unsure of himself) will tend to use some favourite inventory of questions. He will say afterwards, perhaps, 'I asked him about his school-days, his relationship to his parents, his job, his sex life and everything – but we got nowhere.'

Although there can be no useful list of right questions, the counsellor can learn where to direct his sensitivity. In general, he may usefully keep an inner ear cocked for contradictions of feeling and for the denial of contradictions. It is helpful to be alert for opposing factors in a client's emotional life, and to notice where one attitude seems to be so rigidly exaggerated that perhaps its opposite is being unconsciously denied.

Some examples may be useful. For instance, what situations and experiences give his client pleasure or pain, a feeling of fulfilment or a feeling of frustration and impoverishment, confidence and security or anxiety, insecurity and fear; by whom does he feel accepted, loved, valued, cherished and by whom rejected and in what circumstances; when and how does he feel his status enhanced and where and how and by whom does he feel disregarded, belittled, humiliated? In what ways and what circumstances does he get a feeling of supremacy and in what a feeling of defeat? What is he proud of and what ashamed of or guilty about?

All these factors are important to his inner feelings. I have suggested that these are the kind of factors the counsellor will listen for. By that I do not mean he should ask about them. In encouraging his client to talk freely about what is important to him, the counsellor will try to make sense out of all these opposites and see where his client comes in relation to those of them which he has revealed. This is not a comprehensive list, still less a questionnaire. It is an indication of the kind of listening that he can do in order to understand his client more fully and share with him what he can understand. Often he will be wise to share with his client those contradictions that he does not understand. In this way the two of them can begin to elucidate some of the values that are important, even decisive, to the client and which have some close bearing on the difficulties that at present beset him.

It is no good asking direct questions about them because it is the client's half-understood, half-recognized feelings and attitudes that are important. The counsellor cannot tell what these are. Neither can the client. And so they work together to see them more fully. This is the art and skill of counselling (or any other form of relationship therapy), the art of helping people to discover more about themselves. The important word here is 'discover'. It is useless to ask 'What are your feelings about so-and-so?' because if the client really knows what they are it is probable they are not an important aspect of his problem. It is what he does not know that is important and likely to be hampering his judgment and bedevilling his relationships.

This is a woolly and emotional territory in which a counsellor already trained in some precise, technical, authoritative, intellectual vocation may feel understandably at sea and irritated. Feelings are muddled, imprecise, changeable, only partially controllable, partially conscious, often contradictory and unpredictable.

For these reasons it is necessary to indicate how important they are and, so far as possible, to enlist the reader-counsellor's compassion towards a fellow-being in distress. This I will now attempt by what is perhaps a rather peculiar device, inviting the reader to make an imaginative leap into a totally new, totally unforeseen situation, as follows.

Let us suppose that yesterday you had a very serious car accident. That is not a pleasant thought but at least it did not happen. In this accident you were severely but not mortally injured. You have recovered partial consciousness but you cannot speak and are uncertain where you are. You can move a little but not much and you cannot co-ordinate your movements. You cannot see clearly and cannot understand the voices and other noises around you. You have no severe pain, only now and then some troublesome discomfort. You cannot ask for help, do not know exactly who you are. There are movements around you which you cannot fathom. You do not recognize anyone, do not know what they are doing or why. You have no reason to think that anything is going to alter. Things are done to you but you can neither help nor resist. Some of these make you more comfortable, some are unpleasant or painful. Time has no meaning. You do not know whether it is day or night. Nothing is yours, nothing is recognizable, nothing familiar, nothing is possible for you to achieve. You are just about as helpless as one can be.

It is tempting to pass on from this unpleasant thought and see what it is meant to illustrate. But we must not do that yet. We must imagine that no one comes to visit you, you recognize nobody and this goes on and on and on, for days and weeks and months. There is hardly any change, only this shattering experience of helplessness, frustration, pain, alternating with comfort. At last there are two gradual improvements. One is that you become aware there is a bell near one hand and that you can press it. The other is a nurse who looks after you. Sometimes she makes you more comfortable. Sometimes she does things to you that are uncomfortable or painful. Sometimes she understands what you want, sometimes she does not or even misunderstands. Sometimes, worst of all, you ring and she does not come. You ring again and she still does not come. Your pain or discomfort or distress worsens. Eventually she does come.

But sometimes someone else does. This other nurse does not understand your needs. She moves you clumsily, unfeelingly, is careless and uncomprehending. Still you cannot speak or move enough to get comfortable. You are still virtually helpless and unable to communicate. All you can do is ring and hope.

This, as the reader has doubtless guessed, is an imaginative excursion into infancy, the helplessness, dependence, inability to communicate except by crying (bell-ringing), feelings of hunger and fullness, discomfort and frustration. It is not a car accident that did not happen but a situation that did. The parallel is not complete and may be inaccurate in some ways. But at least it will serve to illustrate how basic are our experiences of security, dependence, being cared-for, our primary loneliness and helplessness, our reliance on the care and attention of others.

Can we really doubt that we bring the mark of these experiences into adult life? Have we been kept waiting too long in a restaurant, ignored, our needs not met and do we then not react in a primitive, infantile way, at least inwardly? Do we not tend to regress to infantile feelings and reactions in situations of helplessness, or frustration, or deprivation? Which of us, happily married for a few years, would take kindly to a rival being brought into the home and given more attention than ourselves? Which of us is not threatened inwardly if someone close and dear to us disappears or abandons us or ignores us?

As infants, we had to learn ways of coping with the rough and the smooth of our dependent life, its security and insecurity, its frustration and fulfilment, the presence and the absence of the person on whom we depended for everything. Later, we had to share this person with another, first with father or a brother or sister, then perhaps with a new baby. We had to learn the frustration of not being allowed to satisfy our wants immediately, or do what we wanted to do, having to do what we did not want, to be approved of and disapproved of by the person who was vital to our existence. What happened to the rage we sometimes must have felt towards this vital figure, to the strivings to possess her wholly, to our bodily urges that were not tolerated, to the sources of comfort and satisfaction that were sometimes denied us, to the cries that were not answered, the presence that was not always available when we wanted it?

It would surely be odd indeed if the predicaments of later life did not sometimes reactivate these early experiences, giving us irrational fears and frustrations, joys and comforts out of all proportion to the apparent impact that an outsider might suppose they make on us. Yet many people find it difficult to allow for these primitive reactions in adult life and regard it as humiliating that an intelligent adult may react in emotionally infantile ways.

The precise nature of these reactions is, in individual instances, beyond the concern of the counsellor because the intensity with which such situations are linked is almost wholly unconscious. The psychotherapist is concerned with this area of his patient's experience and he therefore needs a deeper understanding of what is likely to occur during these early years – occurrences that a busy layman may dismiss as irrelevant or fanciful.

It is a useful rule of thumb for the counsellor that emotional attitudes and experiences that stem from periods of life which a client cannot remember are largely inaccessible to counselling. They can only be subject to speculation or theorizing, and both are misleading. But this is not to say that the events in infancy and the experiences which cannot be recalled into consciousness are unimportant. Indeed, they may be crucial factors in the client's development and difficulties. The counsellor would thus be wise to respect and to suspect the bearing of unconscious factors without trying to explore the events and experiences of his client's infancy. This should be left, where it is necessary, to the psychotherapist.

The counsellor, however, can helpfully encourage his client to discuss feelings that he has now, in the complexity of his present situation. This need not (indeed, should not) involve speculative interpretations about infantile parallels or origins. If his client wishes to speak about events of his childhood that he does recall and what connection he feels they may have with his present experiences, well and good. These are unlikely to date back earlier than, perhaps, four or five years of age. The deeper and earlier significance of giving and withholding, good and bad objects, infantile sexuality and fantasy, rage and guilt, and the characteristic responses of the client that stem from these and other early factors may best, for the purposes of coun-selling, be regarded as though they were temperamental or in-born characteristics that can be adjusted to but cannot be modi-fied. They can often be modified, but not by counselling. The counsellor has plenty of useful work to do in discussing the con-scious feelings and experiences, abilities and disabilities, wants, needs and obligations of his client, and in helping him to see what his complex and maybe contradictory feelings are towards people and events in his present situation, without blundering blindfold into the emotionally-charged and irrational area of experiences and feelings repressed in infancy.

The period of the client's life between the age of about five and adolescence may be useful for the light it throws on his present life. During this period he will have rapidly developed his ability to learn, both in an intellectual sense and also emotion-ally by learning to rival others and also co-operate with them, to form friendships and identify himself consciously with admired figures. His social development and the gaining of manipulative skill belong to this period of life and may have an important bearing on how he can relate to other people and the kind of work he can do successfully. In the school years a child normally comes to terms with authority and begins to develop his own character, his sense of moral values. He can express himself cruelly and aggressively, and also lovingly and in friendships. His powers of imagination and his ability to play continue to develop from infancy into the more ordered and conscious ways of childhood. All of these experiences he may be able to recall, and with the counsellor's help he may be able to relate them to his present concerns in ways that had not previously occurred to him.

The emotional turmoil of the twilight stage between child-hood and being grown-up may also be echoed in an adult client's present life. Indeed, some of the turmoil may persist and the attitudes of adolescence remain in being throughout later years. These can sometimes be usefully recognized and discussed in counselling, whereas attitudes persisting from infancy cannot be because they are beyond conscious recall.

Many adult clients who experience sexual troubles can be helped by recapturing the sexual uncertainties of their own adolescent years, the abrupt change from pre-pubertal sexual feelings to physical biological sexual maturity.

Everyone knows today that rebellion against authority (either openly or covertly) and the search for personal identity are normal characteristics of the adolescent years, as are the need for experiment and self-discovery and self-assertion alternating with dependence, the uncertainties of sexual role and personal sexual attractiveness or potency, the defensive alliances against 'the establishment' and the outbursts of defiance and destructiveness, unrealistic but sincere altruism or idealism without practical action.

If the counsellor-reader should feel that this turbulent stage is something that has long passed him by, it is a useful and sobering reflection to notice how many and how close are the parallels between adolescence and middle age.

This breathless gallop through some aspects of personal and emotional development is not intended to do more than alert the counsellor to connections between the present and the past in his client's experience. To be able co-operatively to see what these parallels are does more than simply explain them or help to make sense out of them. The more fully the client can recapture the emotional accompaniments of these earlier experiences, the more fully he is likely (with the counsellor's help) to understand what is happening to him now, what is within his ability and what has always been a problem for him. He has a second chance to come to terms with some challenge, some difficulty, some maladjustment or negative, hostile relationship by (as it were) going over it again with someone who can be trusted and who does not take an unhelpful part against him. An earlier experience is seldom a simple cause of a client's subsequent difficulties in his relationship and is more than an explanation. It is a chance to see the connection more clearly and acceptably, and so find new ways of dealing with it instead of repeating over again a response that only leads him into further difficulty or frustration.

SUMMARY

Counselling and training – experiencing and describing – working through a problem – impact on the counsellor – he is fallible – not simply a mirror – the client tests the counsellor – mutual reactions – the difficulty remains central to the discussion – contrast with psychotherapy – transference – the counsellor's response – causal explanation seldom enough – comparison with social relationships – belief in our own reasonableness – interplay of unconscious feeling – creativity – knowing and knowing about – contradictory feelings – half-recognized attitudes – imaginary excursion into infancy – primitive reactions in adult life – experiences of infancy mainly inaccessible to counselling – events of childhood and adolescence – equivalent of middle age – a second chance for the client.

CHAPTER 8

Interaction

As soon as the interview starts, a counsellor faces the task of assessing relationships and grasping the interaction between conflicting or opposite factors.

The first contrast is usually between the internal and the external (subjective and objective) aspects of the situation. Before the interview can develop there may be urgent and critical problems to face. These may be legal, medical, financial, vocational or connected with social problems such as eviction, rehousing or finding accommodation, according to the context within which the counsellor works.

If a client is ill or if it is uncertain whether he is ill or not, he must see a doctor before the counselling can get very far. If there are legal questions involved in his problem, then these must be attended to by legal advice before the counselling can usefully proceed. If a mother has been left without money to buy the family food or been locked out of her home, if a client is extremely disturbed or suicidal, then such emergencies must take priority over a counselling discussion. No counsellor can responsibly sit back and dismiss them as presenting problems.

However, in making his assessment the counsellor may have difficulty in deciding where priorities lie. He cannot avoid assessing both the reality of the situation and also the way his client sees his predicament and is reacting to it. It is thus necessary for us to consider some of the factors that may help him to form an effective judgment.

Emergencies may arise in which there seems to be no question of counselling for the time being. For instance, a youth leader may have to make an immediate decision on how to deal with a crisis in his club, whether to apply discipline, turn a blind eye, join in or evade the issue. Such judgments are part of his job.

His training will have taught him how to deal with them. Similar issues arise in any institution, a school or borstal institution, a training college or college of further education. In earlier chapters we have considered this type of problem in general terms. We need now to look at it in the particular circumstances of individual interviews.

A counsellor may be faced with a situation that his client regards as just such a crisis, demanding immediate action. Yet after even a brief discussion the counsellor may see that in reality there is no crisis, only a feeling of crisis. The problem is real but the urgency is subjective and its meaning may be obscure. These two aspects need different handling. Sometimes the choice is not easy and the counsellor can but rely on his own judgment. Some clients may be determined on legal action, not so much to correct what is wrong but as the only way they know to express their hostility or anger. Others may fear persecution or some injury from which they demand urgent legal protection, when really the fear is out of all proportion to the risk they are facing. People may demand authoritarian action by a third party because they feel powerless to deal with circumstances themselves. Some are eager to escape from a job or a relationship because they see this as 'the only solution' to what has become intolerable, whereas there may be other options open to them which they cannot recognize as feasible. Others have reached their limit of endurance of pain, discomfort or physical distress although they have been medically examined and reassured that there is nothing wrong and they are not physically ill. Far from satisfying them, this may increase their feeling of desperation and bring them to a counsellor, sometimes indirectly through their resulting incapacity to deal with the normal obligations of life – working, getting the children off to school or fulfilling some social engagement.

We should now consider where the external and the internal (or subjective) aspects meet. This is the factor referred to in earlier chapters as the meaning that the situation or problem has for the individual client.

If a counsellor has been listening attentively and helping his client to express himself and has not been distracted by trying to think up solutions, he can begin to assess what is happening, not with the assurance of a diagnosis but as a clue which the subsequent discussion may begin to follow.

For instance, accompanying a client's outline of his difficulty there may be feelings of anxiety (that is, fear without an exact knowledge of what is causing it) or anger, hostility, aggression or frustration (which is dammed-up activity or emotion).

If the counsellor can help this client to explain what is troubling him, without digressing to a lot of factual or historical matter, then both of them may begin to understand the immediate source of the client's emotional reaction. That is to say, he may feel threatened by something or someone who is putting pressure on him, trying to force him to do something he cannot do or be the kind of person he cannot be. It may be events that produce this pressure – an impending exam perhaps, a test of sexual prowess or ability, a need to keep his temper for fear of losing his job or getting hurt, or being disapproved of or disliked. One cannot be sure how far this sense of pressure may be regarded as normal, or how far it arises from some special vulnerability in this individual to withstand this type of strain. The distinction is not important at this stage. The client's anxiety may be obvious or obscure. If obvious, he will show signs of being threatened by something that he feels powerless to deal with. He is likely to be agitated, hurried, worried, and desperately eager for something to be done at once to relieve him of his burden.

With another client the feeling may be one of tension rather than pressure. He is not so much threatened as unable to meet a challenge, frustrated, held back, unable to express what he wants to express, unable to do or get what he wants and needs, restricted by conditions or by a person, or by the predictably disastrous results of doing something he feels driven to do.

Situations of pressure or tension are relationships. This is seldom obvious at first – certainly not to the client and possibly not to the counsellor, who may be swept along by the intensity of his client's feelings into seeing the problem the way *he* sees it, as arising wholly outside himself, from some external threat or restriction. If the client is to be helped it will not be enough to remove or evade what troubles him. It will be necessary to understand the nature of the relationship between himself and his problem, so that he can find within himself the ability to deal with it more effectively.

Emotional pressure and tension always arise from an interaction. There is pressure acting on someone, tension between opposing forces, emotions, participants. When we say 'This happened to me' we seldom realize the extent to which we may have contributed to it unconsciously. When we do not realize this, we remain vulnerable to that particular type of pressure or tension.

Tension is more obviously double-ended than pressure. Frustration and restriction are obstacles, certainly. But they hinder someone or something, get in the way of something, limit or frustrate somebody. The tension lies between two poles. A tug-of-war comes to an end if one side stops pulling; so does an argument. We are frustrated partly by circumstances but partly by the inflexibility with which we focus all attention on the external barrier (which may be a person rather than a situation). Counselling helps a client to see the other end of the string, that is to say, himself and his own abilities, his vulnerability, that part of his conflict of feeling or motive that he cannot face because he can see only the external barrier in his path.

The threats, challenges, tests and frustrations that beset us are not only double-ended but also symbolical. Their meaning is not literal. Hence the lack of comprehension with which our fears and frustrations may be met by anyone who is unable to grasp their inner meaning – or even the probability that they have an inner meaning for us. This kind of emotional symbolism, so irritating to people who pride themselves that everything is soluble by common sense alone, is at the heart of counselling.

A problem that alarms or frustrates a person may seem trivial to somebody else, even one who knows him well. Then the latter may tell him 'I can't think why you make so much fuss about it.' It is the counsellor's job, however, to try to discover what it *is* about. He may never discover all that it symbolizes, but he and his client may begin to see enough of the background to make a new approach possible.

Anxiety (no matter what situation gives rise to it) may be seen in two ways. It is an alarm-bell ringing from a feeling of danger, and it is potentially a drive towards safety or escape. Because the threat is symbolical as well as literal, our response may be inadequate, or even disastrous – a panic reaction when we have lost control; or our distress may be so great that someone or something intervenes to remove us to safety, to security.

I

Frustration also has two facets. We feel deprived of freedom, of opportunity, activity or self-expression. This arouses our aggression so that we struggle or fight our way out of the difficulty.

Both anxiety and frustration sometimes look like disabilities, symptoms of maladjustment, potentially leading to neurosis or criminality. Both may also sometimes look like attempts at solving a real difficulty. It may be wise and sensible to retreat, to run away from danger just as it may be better, on the contrary, to turn and fight. There are other ways of dealing with difficulties and problems beside these, but anxiety or frustrated aggression is often the force behind them.

It is often said that most of us tend to react to our difficulties in either of two ways – by fight or by flight. Seen in their undesirable aspects these are expressed in delinquency or neurosis (the so-called flight into illness). But they are not necessarily anti-social or sick. There are occasions for fighting and occasions for retreating. The important question is the freedom to choose. Moreover, there are other ways, too, of dealing with our initial reaction to challenges and threats, for instance constructively, co-operatively, courageously (which need not involve a fight so much as facing unpleasantness), creatively by evolving something new and original or by a denial of personal involvement. This last presents difficulties for a counsellor since a client's bland and self-satisfied or defensive-offensive denial of a problem requires considerable skill if it is to be handled helpfully. Frustrated or anxious reactions to problems are much easier for the counsellor since there is, so to speak, a head of steam behind the discussion. There is a motive or drive to get to the bottom of things. But a denial of any part in the difficulty, an inability of the client to see how he himself is, or even might be, a factor in the unstable, painful or unsatisfactory relationship, sometimes leaves a counsellor feeling helpless. Aggressive or hostile feelings may, in such instances, be projected outwards on to someone else who is genuinely felt to be the sole cause of all the trouble. When this happens the client's own part in the situation will not appear as a reaction to pressure or tension, and the counsellor may be unconsciously manœuvred into assuming there is nothing to be achieved with the client, only with some other party whom he blames entirely. Difficult as it is, this situation is not hopeless, for the counsellor may be able to stimulate a discussion on the lines of 'Well, if that is what he does, perhaps we had better try to see what *you* might do about it'. If a basis of co-operation can be established in this way, it may lead to what the client can and cannot do in the relationship and thus to his own involvement in it.

These situations of feeling may arise with clients of any age and in any context, and usually occur symbolically. For instance, anyone may become involved in an intractable situation at work, arising either from personal relationships with superiors, equals or inferiors, or from the significance that the work itself has for the individual. Anyone may find himself in a situation where he is frustrated because he feels his latent energy, ability or ambition do not get adequate scope. So, too, one may be tense and anxious from a feeling of inadequacy in what one is expected to do, to achieve. There may be pressures of possible redundancy, seeing a rival promoted, being moved to another branch or town or having more work put upon one than seems fair or within one's ability.

This type of difficulty may arise in any work situation, at school, in secondary or professional education or training, or in any job, at any age. The symbolism likely to be involved in such problems may be connected with self-satisfaction derived from doing, from activity, ability, competence. Since accusations of incompetence are for most men symbolical accusations of impotence (and vice versa), a client may react with a degree of anxiety, aggressiveness or evasion that at first sight seems incomprehensible until one appreciates the link. This may never emerge in the counselling, because it may be charged with intense emotion that keeps it out of consciousness. But there may be hints, in terminology, unconscious puns or double-meanings, that give an unmistakable hint of intense sexual anxiety behind an apparently purely vocational difficulty.

A woman client is, obviously, not troubled in the same way. For her, problems that arise in work situations and which arouse comparable anxiety or aggression are more likely to be symbolical of depreciation of her as a person – that she is ignored, overlooked, treated as an object. Usually she can compensate for such difficulty by the relationships she makes with workmates or colleagues, which may reassure her and give her a feeling of identity. Similarly male students are commonly disturbed by the prospect of failure, with its implication of inability, and girl students by unsatisfactory personal relationships in their college life.

Personal problems that at first seem to be financial difficulties often turn out to be highly symbolical. They spring from ambition and envy, over-generosity and a compulsive drive to be liked, a need for the security that possessions represent, a desire to please or a need to be flattered, a giving or withholding attitude to someone or to others generally, a need for the extra status and success that come with possession. Money is often unconsciously symbolical of love, of seduction, of appreciation or deprivation, rejection, manipulation.

Sexual problems and situations are perhaps the most highly-endowed of all with unconscious symbolism. Sex is not only a universal drive within the personality and inextricably embedded in mind and body. It is inevitably associated with highly-charged emotional attitudes derived from early life, and part of the childhood emotional atmosphere of love and aggression, valuing and being valued, giving and taking and withholding and (perhaps most important of all) sharing. Difficulties in establishing or re-establishing a mutually-satisfying sexual partnership are seldom matters of sexual technique but of the degree of integration of the amoral, impersonal sexual drive (emotional and physical) with the ability to love, care for and cherish another person. To the extent that a man or woman has been unable to integrate these two aspects of sexuality they will be handicapped in making a sexual relationship that is mutually satisfying, lasting, delightful, rewarding and loving. When sexual problems arise of enough severity to bring a client to a counsellor, the latter is likely to find the counselling to centre around two distinct aspects : firstly, the quality of relationships the client is capable of making, and secondly, the symbolism that sexuality (as a biological and psychological drive) has for him personally. This symbolism is bound to be complex, diverse and is often ambivalent, associated with feelings of love and hate, of dominance and submission, of giving and withholding, of guilt, shame and pride, of punishing and reparation, of achievement and valuing, and of bodily joy and emotional guilt. Money, too, can be associated with these complex feelings and may also express them symbolically, but sex is more deeply embedded in our totality of mind and body.

Sex and money are the two richest aspects of daily life for the unconscious expression of symbolism. Correspondingly, the two categories of counselling that are the most complex and difficult for counsellors are adolescent and marriage counselling. Within them are expressed the two basic tasks of personal living, the establishment of personal identity and the making of a total and complementary relationship with another person. The degree to which we have been handicapped in developing our own identity in adolescence will limit our ability to make a total and unconditional relationship in marriage. Many a severe marital difficulty (no matter in what area of the marriage it first emerges) can be greatly relieved, and the marriage correspondingly stabilized and enriched by a re-enactment of the process of integration that was only partially achieved in adolescence. By re-enactment I do not mean merely talking about it but recapturing the issues of that turbulent time and, at least to some extent, re-living them in the relationship between client and counsellor.

Marital difficulties involve complex issues in which the partner is both idealized and diminished, through the unconscious process by which unacknowledgeable aspects of the one are projected on to the other (and vice versa) and he or she is then blamed for them. It is this aspect of marital interaction that explains the apparent paradox by which a marriage can be helped through counselling with only one of the partners. When he can, with the counsellor's help, take a step forward towards personal integration that was not possible during his adolescence, then he will no longer project his unacceptable characteristics on to his wife. She will find him more tolerant and easier to live with and will respond accordingly. Then he will tell the counsellor how much nicer she has become.

The emotional reorientation of a family with the dawn of puberty is almost as far-reaching and dramatic as the birth of the baby. Indeed, adolescence is a new birth of another kind. Many a harassed and bewildered parent says 'I don't recognize her (or him) any more'. The sexual-biological maturity that comes with puberty is accompanied by a psychosexual reorientation of the family as bewildering for the young person as for his parents. He is now a symbol of the new generation that is to displace the old. Tensions and rivalries deriving from the family triangle (two

sexes and three people) greatly complicate the process of adjustment and, more important, the establishment of a new, sexually
mature individual. Again the young person is in strange sur-
roundings (not literally but psychologically), a stranger among
strangers, a new being in an uncomprehending world, with
unprecedented demands and pressures put upon him at a time
of physical and psychological upheaval. Is it over-dramatic to
compare this to the situation of the infant emerging into a
strange incomprehensible world, or to regard adolescence as in
some ways a second birth?

At any rate, the process of finding his identity is for the
adolescent as necessary and almost as portentous as for the
infant, and in some respects he gets less help. An infant makes
greater physical demands on his parents but he is not a new rival
in the way that an adolescent is. It is often surprisingly difficult
for an adult to establish a useful counselling relationship with
adolescents. The turbulence of their indeterminate role in life
(neither child nor adult), the upheaval caused by their rapid
growth, their difficulties of co-ordination, the onset of sexual
feelings and their physical sexual development, throw them into
a whirlpool of uncertainty and disorientation and lead them
inevitably into all the contradictions and excesses that so
raucously, moodily or unpredictably accompany this stage of
development. Sustained counselling of a formal kind, with a
series of hour-long interviews, is seldom feasible and many well-
meaning attempts to establish such a service have proved unwork-
able. The belief that adolescents are eager to discuss their difficulties with adults if only an opportunity is given them has often
been disappointed. Perhaps this is as well, because such work is
extremely difficult. A few marriage guidance councils have
successfully established such counselling services, but only with
psychiatric support and both basic and in-service training
facilities.

It is the more important that those who work with adolescents
should be alert to the types of situation in which some informal
counselling help may be given when the need arises. That is to
say, where an already existing relationship (such as youth leader
or tutor) may be relied upon as a reference-point for both the
young person and the adult. This enables both of them to use
their relationship tentatively and in direct connection with issues

of an external kind. In adult counselling it is a waste of time always to keep alibis at hand, which may be used to evade tricky or embarrassing issues. But in counselling with adolescents one is wise, as it were, to leave the door open on the encounter. Students in higher (or further) education establishments or training colleges, who have just passed through the adolescent phase, as well as adolescents still at school or in youth clubs, can often be greatly helped by a counselling approach provided it is offered casually (in passing, as it were) and as long as they are not expected to attend a formal interview. The counsellor's skill is the same, but it is applied differently and he may constructively use a situation – some crisis or emergency, some apparently casual incident or topic, some excitable argument or rebellious gesture – in a way that shows by implication rather than explicitly that he is aware of other issues which are being expressed or challenged by implication. He can do this more easily if he knows the student or member personally, in his ordinary role. For his part, he can rely on the assessment of the individual that he has already spontaneously made in the normal run of events. And the young person will also have assessed him and can approach him, so to speak, under the disguise of some overt query rather than having to knock on a door labelled Counsellor. Those who work as counsellor in a more formal setting may need to take time to allow a working relationship with each young person to develop, since both of them have to start from a different footing.

In all varieties of counselling, however, an assessment has to be made of factors which are rigid, fixed and unchangeable, and those that are dynamic and open to modification or adjustment. Between these extremes lies an area of doubt. Is this client an angry aggressive person by nature or temperament, or is this an unwonted reaction to a specially challenging or frustrating problem? Is this unhappy, hopeless person gloomy by nature or is he depressed; or how far is his unhappiness a response to difficulties that would make anyone miserable?

We have dealt with these issues in general terms. They cannot be settled in advance, and we have considered the individual counsellor's own way of seeing issues that confront him. But we have not yet considered the degree to which any client's way of seeing reality is coloured by his past experience.

Sometimes this problem is expressed in a somewhat over-simplified way as 'Nature or Nurture', the assumption being that what is called Nature cannot be modified by counselling (or for that matter by psychotherapy) whereas what is classed as Nurture may be modifiable (at least to some extent) by re-education or working-through the original experiences by recollection.

Inevitably, the counsellor's own past experience also colours his way of seeing reality, that is, the reality of the client who sits by him. Nothing but continuous in-service training (or still better, a period of analytical therapy) can do much to widen the scope of an individual counsellor's empathy, his readiness and ability to share many of his client's uncertainties, his ability to keep his assessments tentative, the essential perceptiveness by which he can sense the possible inner meaning of his client's reactions and discuss them with him.

The way a counsellor puts this perceptiveness at the service of the situation under discussion will determine the degree to which he can help each individual client. He needs to understand personality development, the formation of stereotypes, the earlier experience, and factors likely to be of dynamic significance in their reassessment of the client's problems. And he needs to balance these, so far as he can, against unchangeable features in each client's emotional make-up.

These guesses and tentative perceptions arise out of the counsellor's special role, and from the implications behind what his client tells him about the present problem and about his former experiences. Within this framework the two of them may begin to distinguish issues that are rigid (at least, so far as counselling is concerned) and unchangeable and, on the other hand, those which arise from unconscious emotional responses and which can be shared, looked at afresh and modified. The counsellor's friendly and concerned uncertainty helps his client to find how far some of the apparently fixed reference-points of his life are understandable and modifiable after all.

As the counsellor listens to his client and explores with him the trouble that besets him, he will also be observing how this client expresses himself, the assumptions he is making, the stereo-types and values that he takes for granted, and the issues that seem to cause him anxiety or frustration. He will notice also his client's characteristic way of dealing with difficulties, including the experience of being confronted by a counsellor. Some counsellors notice more of these factors than do others, because of their greater perceptiveness. And all counsellors are more perceptive with some clients than with others. These differences are not so important as the capacity to help the client look at his assumptions, his stereotypes, in new ways – not because these are necessarily more valid, but because they may be. It is always a help to see a wider significance in problems that have become narrowed into a dilemma or conflict of two opposites, provided one really accepts the wider possibilities and does not have them thrust forward with conviction. And it is this same ability to accept wider possibilities that the counsellor's skill and his role can foster in those he helps.

This joint assessment of wider possibilities, this gentle and friendly testing of reality against unreality, of the possible against the impossible, the changeable against the unchangeable, this readiness to see wider symbolical issues behind immediate problems that distress the client, are more important than any rigid division of Nature from Nurture in seeking the origin of the difficulties he has in coping with his problems. The counsellor's role is not to establish certainties. It lies in tolerating and making tolerable the uncertainties of living, the ever-changing interaction of personal relationships seen in relation to the rigidities of response in his individual clients. His aim is to widen the area of responsible choice open to each individual client, to take off the brakes from issues that have got stuck, to look again with his client at experiences which limit the way this client sees the reality of his situation. The degree to which a counsellor can help to bring about this widening depends partly on his ability to accept and clarify the issues involved, and partly on the degree to which the client is able to join in the enterprise.

So much for the significance of any counselling dialogue. What we shall now attempt is to illustrate how it works in practice.

SUMMARY

Urgent problems – priorities and emergencies – a feeling of crisis – demand for action – anxiety, aggressiveness, frustration – tension – symbolism of a challenge – fighting and retreating may be either sensible or compulsive

– denial of a difficulty – projection of aggressive feelings – sexual anxiety in men and women – projection within marriage – counselling with one spouse – adolescence and the family triangle – counselling with adolescents – value of informal help – unchangeable factors – past experiences colour the present – personality development – a client's assumptions and stereotypes – joint assessment of possibilities – making uncertainties tolerable.

CHAPTER 9

A Counselling Interview and Commentary

Tape-recordings enable groups or individuals to study an interview with all its nuances, hesitations, contradictions and changes of emotional tone that form so important an aspect of counselling. The more usual case history depends on memory and is inevitably distorted in the writing, whereas the tape misses nothing and distorts nothing. Moreover passages can be repeated and, by means of transcription, one can study in detail the subtleties that may be missed by both participants at the time and even by anyone hearing a tape played straight through. Such recordings provide an unrivalled chance to observe the interaction between two people as it actually occurred, not as sifted through the memory of one of them or by an observer. Overtones and implications can be recognized unmistakably in a carefully punctuated transcription.

In the present chapter we shall use a transcription to illustrate and summarize aspects of counselling that have been covered in previous chapters. This will enable the reader to clarify his reaction to the important but evanescent impact that two people make upon one another in an interview. The interview was recorded and is reproduced with the knowledge and permission of the two people.

Any first interview is exploratory. The two participants take time to sum up each other and to establish a mutually acceptable way of communicating. They have, as it were, to establish each other's identity and build up enough mutual confidence to make discussion fruitful. For the counsellor, a first interview is relatively easy. He is mainly listening and helping his client to talk. Both of them form an opinion about the value of continuing. The counsellor may explain what he has to offer and may have to face the client's disappointment that he has no immediate and easy solution. Provided he is confident of the (real though limited) value of such a discussion, he will offer a further meeting.

The second interview is much more tricky. Indeed, it is often decisive in how far the client and counsellor are willing and able to go in tackling the difficulty besetting the client. For the present purpose, therefore, a second interview has been chosen. It is short (lasting twenty-five minutes) and is unusually free of repetition or digression. It was a difficult interview for both of them. It is reproduced complete and unaltered. It has been selected for these reasons and not as a model or ideal.

We shall first consider the problem that the client brought to the counsellor. Then we shall hear the counsellor's account of the first interview, so that we can assess how he reacted to the client and her problem. After this, we shall hear the interview itself and consider what happened in it. Finally (in the Appendix) there is a more detailed analysis of the interview, which would unduly interrupt the text if included in this chapter.

First, then, the client's problem in its simplest terms.

The Problem

A wife has two daughters. She wants to know whether she ought to divorce her husband or not. He drinks, spends almost all his evenings in the pub and takes little or no interest in her or his home.

That is the situation she outlined to the counsellor (a man). What impact does it make on the reader? Anyone interested in counselling would probably feel we do not yet know enough to make any valid comment.

But perhaps beneath this hesitation may lie some spontaneous reaction arising from knowledge, experience, conviction about drink, about men who stay away from home in the evening, who take little interest in home, children or wife, about divorce as a remedy or its effect on children, about a wife who cannot see any other solution than to break up her marriage. Or one might wonder whether there are valid grounds on which a divorce petition might succeed. She has not, apparently, asked whether she *can* divorce her husband but whether she ought to. Would it perhaps be better for the daughters if the marriage broke up?

However, there is no obligation to find an instant answer to the problem. A counsellor has the chance to learn more about it before answering, because he can ask questions. And in such a far-reaching problem as a possible divorce the client would probably be willing to answer as much as we want to ask her.

What questions would be relevant if we are to advise her whether she ought to divorce him? We know little, as yet, about the bare facts of the situation, for example, her age, her husband's and the daughters' ages, how long they have been married, their jobs, their home, interests and ambitions, whether they intend to have more children. One might also ask her individual, personal questions about whether she has other complaints against him, what sort of person he is, her views on the morality of divorce (since she asks a moral question) or of drinking, how they get along together in other ways, sexually, financially, at home, in leisure activities, whether there are frequent quarrels, any violence, their state of health, who takes the lead in what, who decides.

It would not be difficult to ask many such questions, before answering her. Indeed, if one is eventually going to say whether or not she ought to divorce him, one should clearly consider as many relevant factors as are available. However, it will scarcely be necessary to remind the reader that this has little to do with counselling. Her moral query shows how she sees her predicament. Sooner or later, she must answer it for herself. Why can she not do so now?

We will not consider how the counsellor might or should deal with this situation. We shall hear how he actually did deal with it. The following is his description of the first interview, recorded directly after it. As soon as the client had left he spoke into the recorder as follows.

a I have seen this client once. I don't think it was a very satisfactory interview for either of us. She began by wanting to know whether she should divorce her husband or not. Whether it was right to divorce him. The reason was that he drinks. During the interview she once or twice called him a drunkard. But the picture really was more of someone who stays out in the evening, goes to the pub, comes back and is just not interested in his home or in her.

b She told me she insists that every Friday he should stay in and not go to the pub, and this he does. But unfortunately it doesn't work out any better. She asks friends in, but he is bored and in fact he even dozes off and goes to sleep in his chair while the friends are there.

c They have two daughters apparently and there was a picture of the three of them (the wife and her two daughters) dressmaking together and in a way quite glad to have father out of the way, at the pub. She told me that her parents were teetotallers, that they felt rather strongly about drink, but that when she was an adolescent she used to feel it was rather dashing to have a drink. She used to go out to dances and have quite a gay time and would have a beer or two. When she got engaged to this chap, they used to go out quite a bit together. The picture was of quite a happy sort of time, she even used to go to the pub with him. But now she is quite convinced that drink is at the root of all her unhappiness.

d She despises her husband I think and one of the reasons she gave for this was that he has no hobby (she felt strongly about this) except, she said, politics. And it was quite obvious that she felt this was not really a man's occupation. It's nothing (she said) but talk, talk, talk, you don't *do* anything, you don't *make* anything, and she seemed quite angry.

e Well, I found her a slow and difficult client, not much response, rather tied up perhaps, bored, I don't know, possibly a little bit depressed. At any rate I certainly found the interview heavy going and I think she did. I tried to see if we could find a way into her problem by asking her (not quite in this way, but substantially this) whether she finds him boring because he drinks, or on the contrary whether perhaps he goes out drinking because *he* is bored. She said again without any hesitation, that drink was at the bottom of all their troubles and that that was that. But the point really was (she felt) is it morally correct or incorrect, right or wrong, to divorce him?

f Well, to be candid, I don't much look forward to this second interview and I am very doubtful, really, whether I can do much to help her. She seems so shut in, in this rather moral, rather self-righteous, perhaps even smug attitude, and with very

little sort of understanding or even *possibility* of understanding
that he too may have some difficulty.

Comments on the counsellor
*If the reader is willing, it would pay him to pause at this point
and record his comments on what the counsellor has just said,
jotting down whatever occurs to him or speaking into a tape
recorder. It would be even better to share comments with others
interested in counselling. The following questions might form the
basis of further discussion.*

How much factual detail (age, income, occupation and so on)
has the counsellor mentioned?

What impression has he given of the relationship between
himself and this client?

What are his feelings towards this woman and her problem?

To what extent does the question of drink seem to affect the
client's and the counsellor's view of her problem?

Does her view of her difficulty differ from the counsellor's?

What does she expect from the counselling and what is the
counsellor willing (or unwilling) to provide?

How may her opinion of her husband's behaviour affect the
way she sees the counsellor?

What words does the counsellor use to describe her? What is
his opinion of her?

In what mood does he approach the second interview?

What does the reader imagine to be the client's feelings about
the interview and about the counsellor?

What factors make it difficult for this client to make up her
mind?

What is her attitude towards her husband and towards the
difficulty she is in, so far as one can guess from what the
counsellor has said?

The counsellor began by admitting what he felt about the interview (para. *a*) and later (para. *f*) how he regards the prospect of
the next one. He contrasts his picture of the situation with hers
(para. *a*). He thinks she is quite glad to have her husband out of
the way sometimes (para. *c*), although this is what she complains about (para. *a*). Her parents were teetotallers but in

adolescence and when engaged she did not follow their example (para. *c*). She scoffs at her husband for talking instead of doing – and that is how the counsellor behaves, he listens and talks but does nothing. What is her reaction to her husband's hobby of talking politics (para. *d*)? The counsellor suggested how her husband might be feeling (para *e*). How did she respond to this? Does he takes sides at all? Finally, what does the reader feel about the counsellor's attitude to this client and to her husband?

Such factors are crucial to progress in the next interview. Because the counsellor has been willing to speak frankly about this first meeting we can see that he is not wholly neutral or uninvolved. He does not tell us what he thinks is the 'solution' to her difficulty or whether he thinks she should divorce her husband, even though this is apparently what she came to find out. He has painted a picture of a relationship as he sees it, in which facts such as age, occupation and income play little part. He has described parts of the interview that tell something about the relationship between this woman and her husband and (to a small extent) her daughters. But this is as he (the counsellor) sees it. It is not (and cannot be) factually objective for it is concerned with values and opinions. By implication, he tells us a good deal about his attitude towards her. One wonders what he would have written in his notes if, instead of speaking informally and off the cuff, he had written a conventional case history. Like clients, counsellors bring more to light when they speak freely than if constrained to be precise and formal. Speaking freely into a tape-recorder directly after an interview is therefore more useful for training than writing formal notes. Case recording for someone else to read can easily lead to following the official line and saying what is expected, jargon and all, whereas recording spontaneously brings one face to face with the realities of the relationship. These can easily pass unnoticed or unrealized if one is trying to develop a technique instead of understanding the interaction between client and counsellor.

We do no know what this client thought about that first interview, but we shall see something of this from the way she begins the next one. But we may guess what she might have said about it. Of course, we can only do this from what the counsellor has told us and she might see it differently from him.

How would the reader suppose she would describe it? My own guess would be something like this: 'I went to ask a straightforward question but he never answered it. I felt free to talk, but got nowhere. I have got to *do* something, not just talk. And I want to know what I am to do, what it is *right* to do, in my circumstances. He was quite nice but he wasn't really any help.' Since we already know how the counsellor feels about the prospective second interview we can pass on to see what they actually said to each other. (It is best to read the interview straight through. The numbered paragraphs will make reference simple when we come to comment on it.)

1   I nearly didn't come back today.
2   Yes?
3   Unless you think that you can tell me . . . what one does, if one has to go on.
4   You mean, how to go on with *him*?
5   Yes.
6   Did you feel last time, that really you hadn't been helped? You came asking my opinion on whether divorce was right, and really and truly I didn't tell you? Did that rather disappoint you?
7   Yes, because that is what I came *for*.
8   Yes. We talked I think of two things really, a little bit about divorce, and secondly about your husband's drinking. But what you want to know now is not quite the same. It is more how it is possible to continue, is that right?
9   Well yes, I think so, because it seems impossible to me. And I thought, well, you said, that you didn't know if it would be any better or not, quite apart from whether it is right or wrong. So I thought well, perhaps I'd better see, think, ask the children.
10 Yes?
11 Do you think I *ought* to ask the children?
12 Ask them what?
13 If it would be a good idea.
14 To divorce him?
15 Yes.
16 You haven't asked them yet?
17 Oh no.

K

18 Do you think perhaps it might be better to get your own feelings a bit clearer before tackling *them* on it?

19 Yes. Well, what I have tried to do, you see, is to think.

20 Yes?

21 Now, what is going to happen to them?

22 Yes?

23 And it didn't seem after all . . . quite such a good idea, because I don't know what would happen.

24 Yes?

25 I don't know, I suppose *I* would get them, wouldn't I?

26 Well, I think there are two points we ought to look at here. One, I can't say whether you would or not. These things depend *not* on who is considered to be guilty of any offence against the partner in marriage, but which is best for the children, do you see? That is the first point. The second (which I think is perhaps a rather important one) is that I'm not at all sure that you *could* divorce him, you see? What do you think you would divorce him *for*?

27 Well . . . well, perhaps not a divorce. Well, I don't want to leave him because I don't want to leave the house.

28 Yes?

29 So I would have to say to him, Go. Which is a bit difficult, isn't it?

30 Why is it difficult?

31 Well, it's *his*, after all.

32 Yes?

33 And if anyone is going, I suppose *I* ought to go.

34 Because the house is his, or for any other reason?

35 Well it's *all* his.

36 Yes?

37 Isn't it?

38 I am not quite sure what you mean, it's all his. The house I suppose is his, is that right, and the things in it, but the marriage isn't *his* really, is it? It's both of you.

39 Well, it wouldn't be there.

40 If he left, it wouldn't – you mean?

41 Or if I left.

42 Do you *want* it to be there?

43 Well, I don't know. That's what is so difficult, I think.

44 Yes?

45 I thought well, obviously I must . . . stop it, change it, make it different, you know? I can't see that *he* can get any different.

46 Yes?

47 Because it's gone on so long.

48 I have the impression you see, that you feel rather hopeless about the whole situation, but even more hopeless about *him*. That it's beyond the bounds of possibility that he can become any happier than he is. Is that so? Or have I got you wrong?

49 Oh I don't . . . yes . . . I think that is so. I don't think I would have put it like that. What I mean is I don't think he'll ever change.

50 Yes?

51 I mean, I don't think he is particularly unhappy is he?

52 Well, the picture you gave me the last time we met didn't strike *me* as a picture of a happy husband. . . . Do you think he is?

53 Well, who is?

54 You don't think any husbands are happy?

55 Well, anybody grown up. . . .

56 Yes?

57 And so on. It never comes out quite right, you know.

58 Yes?

59 But what I mean is, it's going to go on and on and on. And I don't *like* it.

60 You don't think there is anything you can do to change it?

61 No, he'll never change.

62 Why are you so sure of that?

63 Well he's been like this for years and years and years.

64 Have you tried to change it?

65 Oh it's no good. I mean, there is just things that he can't do, and things that he can do, and that's that. And it's always been the same.

66 You don't seem awfully close to each other. Have you *ever* been?

67 . . . I don't know, I suppose . . . yes, yes, I think so. I don't know what happens. All sorts of things are much more fun when they are new, aren't they?

68 Yes.

69 And I suppose one just settles down. There were all sorts of things we did together when we were young. It isn't that he wants to do them, and I don't, or the other way round. It's just that we don't either of us do those kind of things any more.

70 And how do you think that came about? Partly as you say that the – I suppose setting up home and that kind of thing. It's much more fun at first. It can't go on being exciting as it is to begin with. Is there anything else that's made – that's taken the polish off it?

71 Well no, I suppose really you see the thing is that I thought that he *would* change.

72 Did you think that you would change him?

73 . . . Yes. Yes, yes I suppose so.

74 Yes? And then gradually you found you couldn't, and that he didn't change? How did you react to that?

75 Well, you just have to put up with it, don't you?

76 You gave up trying d'you mean?

77 Oh yes, because I mean it's no good . . . just going on and saying Do these kind of things. You know?

78 Are you talking now of his drinking, or of his not being really interested in you and your daughters?

79 Well, I don't think really he is all that domestic is he?

80 No?

81 And I suppose I can't imagine someone who isn't.

82 Sorry, I don't quite get that.

83 Well, I don't see what anybody wants to get married *for*.

84 Unless they are domesticated?

85 Well, not domesticated. Unless they want to look after a home and a family. I suppose it's more comfortable.

86 What's more comfortable?

87 I mean, it's more comfortable for a *man* if he gets married.

88 Than if he stays single?

89 Yes. Then I suppose it's – it's – I don't know – I suppose the only thing is, one just goes on. Does one?

90 I think you can't see that you matter to him. Is that right?

91 Oh I'm all right, by myself.

92 Do you matter to him, do you think? Does he *care* about you?

93 ... I ... yes ... I don't know ... I suppose so. It's all so *dead*, you know.

94 Yes. And your feelings for *him*, they are dead perhaps?

95 Well, of course I don't feel what I used to feel when I was young, but nobody does, do they? You can't expect to go on feeling like that all the time.

96 What do you feel towards him, now?

97 Well, I just feel I have to put up with him, don't I? I think that is a mistake I have made. I daresay, I think lots of people do. I think lots of people do make it. You know, thinking this person that I am going to marry will be different, after some time. And then they aren't and then you just have to put up with it. I mean, you see it all round you. Don't you?

98 I think there is another way of looking at it. I don't know how you think of this. If one's living as close to some-body (as one inevitably is, in marriage) I am not quite sure that *either* can change without the other also changing. Do you think that's so? You see, you talk as if only *he* has changed.

99 I don't ... think so. I said I have changed. I said I didn't want to do these kind of things that we did when we were young.

100 Yes?

101 And I don't expect him to change. But what sort of a change should *I* do? I ... I ... what do I do *wrong*?

102 Did I say you do anything wrong? Do you think you do anything wrong?

103 Well, you said I'd got to change.

104 Did I? What I was trying to say, at any rate, was that in marriage the two partners must quite inevitably react on each other, do you see?

105 Hmm.

106 And that perhaps as time has gone on, your attitude towards him has changed, just as you feel *his* towards *you* has changed. Is that so?

107 Oh yes, that kind of change, yes.

108 Do you feel that any change in *your* feelings for him has been entirely due to his drinking?

109   Well, I think it's got an awful lot to do with it. I mean, he wouldn't be like that if he didn't drink, would he?

110   Like what?

111   Well uninterested and falling asleep, and not bothering about things, and being late and. . . .

112   Well I am not so sure, you see. I mean, after all you see it can only be guess work on my part, can it? But I wonder sometimes whether people drink because they feel unwanted.

113   . . . But it's . . . what . . . but . . . he isn't.

114   He isn't what?

115   Unwanted.

116   Well, unloved?

117   Well you can't just go on and on, without getting anything back can you?

118   . . . Oh, did you feel that he never returned your love for him?

119   Oh no, when we were young it was all right, I think.

120   Yes, yes, and then?

121   Well no, I suppose I am unfair really, I don't know, you see, how much of this is just normal, that you get bored with your husband, and you get bored with your wife, and how much is because he goes on in this awful way.

122   Hmm.

123   I mean is it – sometimes I think well, everybody is like that, and one must just put up with it and realize that all these things you thought when you are young just don't happen really.

124   Perhaps what really matters is whether one kind of loses heart and gives up trying, do you think?

125   You can't really *try* you know, can you?

126   Hmm.

127   I mean either you feel something, or you *don't*, don't you think so? You can't *try* to feel this that and the other.

128   It depends I suppose whether one's marriage means anything to you, you see? I agree that I don't see how one can try to feel something that one doesn't feel, but one can perhaps either continue to try to make one's marriage a better one, or give up in despair, as a sort of stalemate.

129 Well how do you *try*, I mean there isn't much scope is there?

130 Perhaps that's what he feels. Perhaps that's why he drinks.

131 Well what sort of scope should he want that isn't there? The scope's there, but he won't bother.

132 I don't quite understand about won't bother. Can you explain that?

133 Well I'm there, and he's not there, you see. Well you can't go fussing round someone who isn't *there*.

134 And how do you think he feels when he is there? When he does come back, he comes back on Fridays, he comes back for his supper. What does home mean to him?

135 I suppose somewhere where he goes to get some food.

136 Is that *all* he gets there?

137 I don't know. . . .

138 I have the feeling you know that in some way you are very hurt and very angry with him, and that it isn't because of the drink entirely. And I can't see at all where this began. But I think it must have begun somewhere. You know, I don't mean just on one particular Thursday afternoon or something, but it seems to have been building up, as though – because you have been hurt, you felt 'Well I shan't try. I don't care.' And then perhaps he's gone on and on and he thinks 'Well all right, I'll stay out three nights, four nights, five nights, six nights a week'. You know, a sort of vicious circle. Do you think that is what has been going on?

139 Well, it's what happened in a way. Because he didn't go when we were first married, go to the pub like that.

140 Hmm.

141 Well, he used to go occasionally and I used to go with him, but then when the children came I couldn't.

142 Do you think this was the turning point, the arrival of the children?

143 Well I suppose so, you know, one wants something I suppose different when somebody's a father.

144 Will you explain that?

145 Well, I mean that if you are just going to be the two of you like that, it is more – it's easier to have time, isn't it?

146 Before there are children? Oh yes.

147 But if a father doesn't take much interest in a home, or children, and the wife is there all the time, then it is a bit – different. You can't go out together much.

148 Hmm.

149 He did as you said, I think, he went out more and more and more by himself, having gone once, and then one or two evenings a week and then more and more until in the end I had to say 'Well we must have *one* evening when I know you are coming home'.

150 Hmm. Did you both want to have children?

151 Oh yes.

152 Did he want a son?

153 Oh it would have been nice, yes.

154 You too would have liked one?

155 Oh yes.

156 One of each, do you mean, or a son to start with?

157 Oh well I mean, I think it's nicer to have a boy and then a girl, but I wouldn't have minded which way round. But it is nice to have two different ones, isn't it?

158 Hmm. What do you think about him, what did *he* want?

159 Well of course he wanted a boy, I suppose in a way, more than I do – did.

160 Hmm. Did he rather resent your having to spend so much time with the baby, the first one?

161 I don't think so.

162 Hmm.

163 I mean he had his things to do and I had my things to do.

164 But until then you *had* done things together.

165 Oh yes. Not anything very special. I mean we didn't go climbing mountains, or ring bells.

166 Hmm.

167 Or do any of these things, that people say 'Oh yes we've always had this thing in common', you know.

168 Hmm. Did you like to be together?

169 Yes, yes . . .

170 What did he mean to you in those days, do you think, before your first daughter was born?

171 I suppose a kind of companion.

172 You felt that he was a kind of companion to you?

173 Yes, not the sort of old-fashioned one.

174   Somebody to do things with?
175   Yes.
176   Hmm. Can you describe your feelings towards him in those days?
177   No, you see it is all finished really, isn't it? I mean it's different now. It is no good thinking about things like that.
178   You mean this is a subject you don't want to go into.
179   Well I don't see why. You can't go back again, can you?
180   Shall I tell you why, why I asked you this?
181   Yes.
182   I asked you, you see, because I think that often one's basic feeling towards the person who matters most in one's life doesn't really change as it may seem to change. And if one gets hurt and unhappy one sometimes feels that everything is hopeless and it is almost too painful to look back and see what really one's feelings are for him underneath. Do you see? That's why I asked you. I wanted to know if you were able to take a look back and see if it isn't still possible to – well, not to put the clock back but to recover some of those feelings that might still be there. Do you see?
183   Yes. Yes, I see what you mean.
184   These things are complicated, aren't they? . . . I think you said, did you say, you would have to stop at half-past?
185   Yes.
186   Because it's about a couple of minutes until then. Well, now I don't – you see I haven't again given you any direct answer, have I?
187   No, but I don't think I can just go off, can I?
188   Go off and leave him?
189   Hmm.
190   I think it would be an awful pity yet. It is going to uproot the family, it is going to mean many complications, isn't it, financial and otherwise, goodness knows how your daughters will feel. I don't think it need necessarily be quite such a stalemate as I think you feel it is now.
191   Well, what do I do?
192   I think it might be worth while, you know, if we could have a little more time together, and look into your feel-

ings towards him and his towards you. But you are not very
keen on that, are you?
193   Well I could *think* by myself.
194   Yes. Then would you like to come along or would you be
willing to come along and tell me what you thought?
195   Yes.
196.   Right. Thank you.

To get the most from this short interview, the reader would be
well-advised, as before, to write (or record or share) his own
comments before reading further.

The remarks and questions which now follow are not intended
to be didactic but to offer a basis for further discussion or consideration.

The client's problem
What are the simplest terms in which one might describe this
client's difficulty? After the first interview, it appeared to be
whether she ought to divorce her husband because he drinks
and spends most evenings at the pub. What does it seem to be
now?

Perhaps one can summarize what she has said in this way:
'My situation is hopeless. My husband doesn't care a bit about
me or his marriage or the family. All it means to him is comfort
and food. He will never be different. Therefore I must either
put up with it or break up the marriage. Which is it to be?'

Expressed as a dilemma or conflict, her problem might be
put like this: 'My marriage is dead. There are only two possibilities, to put up with it or break it up, since he will never change.
But I can't put up with it, because it is so awful. And I can't
break up the marriage because of the children and because the
home is all his.'

And she wants the counsellor to tell her which to do.

What does his response amount to? Perhaps we can summarize it in these words: 'Is it correct to assume your marriage
is dead and there is nothing you can do (or be) to revive it?
I realize you feel hopeless about it but I don't understand why.
Were things always as bad as this? If not, when and how and
why did they begin to go wrong? If we can understand this,

we may see it in a different light. Putting up with it may not be the only alternative to breaking it up. Let us try to see more clearly what is going on in you and also in the relationship with your husband and children.'

Her marriage

We can use her own remarks to show how she sees her marriage. For instance, 'It is *all* his' (35), 'It's more comfortable for a *man* if he gets married'(87), 'It's all so *dead*' (93), 'Somewhere he goes to get some food' (135). This is a gloomy picture of marriage and it implies that she plays no essential part in it, there is no living relationship, she has no stake in it and feels taken for granted. This hopeless attitude is reflected in other remarks.

Her despair

This attitude emerges unmistakably throughout the interview. After their first interview it led the counsellor to describe her as slow and difficult, not much response, bored and perhaps a bit depressed.

In the second interview she expresses the same attitude clearly. For instance 'I can't see that *he* can get any different' (45), 'It never comes out quite right, you know . . . It's going to go on and on and on. And I don't *like* it' (57, 59), 'Oh it's no good. I mean, there is just things that he can't do, and things that he can do, and that's that' (65), 'Well you can't just go on and on, without getting anything back can you?' (117), 'There isn't much scope is there?' (129), 'The scope's there, but he won't bother' (131) and the resigned comment 'No, you see it's all finished really, isn't it?' (177).

No wonder the counsellor found this client difficult. A feeling of defeat, hopelessness, despair, depression is always difficult to help. A counsellor may, as it were, catch it and feel defeated also. Then he may say afterwards 'Nothing I suggested was any good'.

Positive feelings

In spite of the prevailing gloominess of her attitude, there are signs that this is not quite the whole picture. She cares about the children and what may happen to them. Indeed, this is something which apparently did not enter into the first interview. In spite of what the counsellor said about it, perhaps it was not such a failure if it led her to see her problem even this much more widely. At any rate, she now says '. . . quite apart from whether it is right or wrong. So I thought well, perhaps I'd better see, think, ask the children' (9).

Even though she makes a sad contrast between early marriage and the later stages she says 'I don't know what happens. All sorts of things are much more fun when they are new, aren't they?' (67). The word 'fun' (even though referring to the past) comes unexpectedly from this client. Even the despairing remark already quoted, about going on and on and getting nothing back (117), implies that marriage *can* be more than just a husband's comfort and food. And about halfway through the interview she remembers a happier time. 'He didn't go when we were first married, go to the pub like that. Well, he used to go occasionally and I used to go with him' (139, 141). The counsellor may have been tempted to ask her 'Well, why don't you now?'

Indeed (just before this), when the counsellor suggests her husband may be feeling unwanted, she is obviously taken aback by a new idea and cannot answer for a few moments. Then she makes a hesitant but telling reply '. . . But it's . . . what . . . but . . . he isn't' (113). And she says, a little later, 'When we were young it was all right' but she quickly adds 'I think' (119).

Further positive feelings emerge towards the end of the interview. She replies unhesitantly that both of them wanted children (151) and that she wouldn't have minded whether a boy or girl came first. And she even describes her husband as having been 'a kind of companion' (171) in the early days. Even the most hopeless remark of all about its being 'all finished really' (177) ended with the question 'Isn't it?' Complete despair would not ask. The little question is perhaps less a shimmer of hope than a call for help.

Evaluation

It is valid to ask about any interview 'What did it achieve?' The difficulty about answering is that anyone will judge it by his own assumptions about counselling. One could say of this second interview (as we confidently said of the first, as did the client herself) that the counsellor did not advise her on whether it was right to divorce her husband. He did, however, query whether she had the grounds and she seemed to take this as a chance to show that she is no longer seriously considering it as a possible answer (26, 27).

What was he aiming at during this interview? There were a few direct comments from the counsellor. He summed up their first interview briefly (8), he explained about custody of children and grounds for divorce (26), he queried her one-sided view of the marriage (98) and whether drink was the whole explanation (108), he brought up the question of how her husband may be feeling (134), he asked whether both of them wanted children (150) and he even went so far as to say it would be an awful pity to break up the marriage yet, because it may not be quite such a stalemate as she thinks (190), and finally he adroitly (or perhaps a little smartly) invites her to return for further discussion (194). Smart or adroit, she agrees with the suggestion.

So much for the direct aspects of the counsellor's comments. They are not authoritative, saying or hinting what she should or should not do or be. But they are positive. Indeed, counsellors who are committed to wholly non-directive techniques would criticize him for taking too active a part in the discussion.

There is, however, another scale of values that can legitimately be applied to the interview. This is to consider the feeling aspect, since this is the area in which counselling can be of most use.

The client's opening remark is a most telling start. (Incidentally it is also a striking example of the wisdom of a wait-and-see attitude in counselling.) Some conventional greeting or routine query or casual introduction about the weather or the news might have made it impossible for her to bring this remark in its full impact.

What impression does it give the reader? What do people mean when they tell us that they 'nearly' did something? They didn't do it, but they 'nearly' did. What is the significance, why is it worth saying?

At the start of this interview there is a first phase in which they are discussing her expectations and her disappointment that he did not tell her what to do and now (3) she gives him a second chance.

After this start, the next phase mainly expresses her prevailing hopelessness, with the counsellor trying to bring out into the discussion what she feels. At 89 she virtually repeats her opening remark, saying in effect 'Look, have I have just got to stick it out, or what?' bringing the counsellor back to her demand for a decision : 'One just goes on, does one?' (89). By common-sense, extroverted standards the counsellor makes an odd reply, 'I think you can't see that you matter to him. Is that right?' (90) to which she makes (by the same standard) an even odder reply 'Oh I'm all right by myself' (91). They now begin to discuss the interaction of feeling within the marriage. For the first time she is unmistakably angry (101) but accepts the counsellor's explanation that he was not implying a criticism (106, 107). They pursue the topic of what husband and wife mean to each other and she vividly expresses her anger at being rejected 'You can't go fussing around someone who isn't *there*' (133). The counsellor keeps to this topic. pressing her about her attitude to her husband until she can reply no further. There is a silence and she says weakly 'I don't know . . .' (137).

Here the counsellor attempts a clarification of what they have so far discussed and she accepts it (138, 139). And they now begin to discuss what went wrong and when it was. In this phase she has become more readily co-operative and less hopeless, and they are working together. This has probably become possible because his clarification showed that he understood her predicament. But when he tries to continue with her earlier feelings towards her husband (after she said he was a companion) her feeling of defeat suddenly returns and she refuses, saying 'It is no good thinking about things like that' (177). The counsellor accepts this criticism of what he was doing and explains himself (182). She replies 'Yes. Yes, I see what you mean' (183).

He then looks at his watch since she has apparently said that her time was limited to half-an-hour or so (incidentally, this may be a way of expressing her mixed feelings towards him and the counselling). They discuss as colleagues her possible leaving of her husband. She makes the final challenge 'I could *think*, by myself' (193) which (perhaps mistakenly) the counsellor takes to mean 'No more counselling, thank you'. He invites her to come back, perhaps a little brusquely, but the interview is over and she must go.

In the Appendix we shall look in more detail at some of the implications underlying these exchanges, and the interaction between counsellor and client in relation to her problem.

To conclude this general consideration of the interview, the reader might care to make his own assessment in relation to the general characteristics of a counselling interview listed in Chapter 6. They can be re-phrased as questions, thus :

1 To what extent did the counsellor put pressure on the client to hurry her or bring her to the point quickly? Was he anxious in himself or was he adequately unhurried? Did he bring authoritative or expert pressure on her, pass moral judgment or try to persuade her in any direction? And how did she respond?

2 Did he accept her problem as valid not only as a literal problem but in relation to the underlying feelings expressed in it? How far did he succeed in sensing her predicament or did he regard it as incomprehensible or making an unnecessary fuss?

3 Was he able to help her clarify the meaning that her problem has for her, to see it more clearly both in its external or environmental aspects and its internal, emotional aspects? Were they able to share their views co-operatively?

4 Was the counsellor able to grasp her underlying feelings towards her husband and her marriage (and towards him) and could he tolerate the part they play in her relationships? Could he accept what she inwardly feels? Did he appreciate how she cannot be expected to overcome her difficulties without taking these inner feelings into account and coming to terms with them?

5 What uncertainties or contradictions in the client's feelings arise during the interview or are implied in it? How far is the counsellor able to accept them as valid for her and not absurd or contradictory because inconsistent or inconstant? What opposing factors may be contributing to her inability to cope with the estrangement that has arisen between them, to her original concern about his drinking as the basis of their disharmony and yet a factor she scarcely mentions in the second interview, only referring to it in answer to a question (109)? What are her basic feelings towards her husband and towards the counsellor? Does the counsellor accept both her co-operation and her hostility, her demands and her dependence, her hopelessness and her demand for advice?

6 How far does the counsellor accept or reject her as a person? As her feelings become clearer does he change his attitude towards her? Does he actually or implicitly praise or blame her?

There can be no precise answers to these questions. Indeed,

this short interview illustrates how imprecise and shifting a job this is. Nevertheless, we should ask such questions and make such evaluations, however tentative and individual they may be. Only by doing so can one gradually clarify one's own mind in relation to what can be attempted in a counselling discussion. The actual ability to do it can come only from practice and experience and from whatever chances one may have to discuss the work with others.

Finally, this short interview illustrates how slow and tentative counselling often is. The only progress is towards a deeper and franker level of communication between her and the counsellor. Whatever else the counsellor did or failed to do, he recognized the importance of this factor. To have tried to press on towards making up her mind or even assessing the marriage more fully (by asking about other aspects of it than she has mentioned) would have done nothing towards establishing a working basis.

Unless her feeling of defeat can be recognized and brought into the open it will remain a barrier to any further co-operation, let alone progress. Even in the interview it arose as a final defence against further discussion. It is as well, therefore, that the counsellor did not feel as hopeless as she did and was able to bring out this stumbling-block into their discussion. She responded helpfully because, for the moment at any rate, she felt her difficulties were understood.

If her relationship with her husband is to get on to a fuller and more mutually-rewarding basis, further interviews will be necessary, possibly many more. And it is likely that there will be stormy times ahead in future interviews as she is able to come nearer to her uncertainty about her own value and her feeling that she is powerless to meet others (at any rate, other men) on equal terms. The less conscious aspects of her disability will be considered briefly in the Appendix.

SUMMARY

Use of tape-recordings – observing interaction – a first interview is exploratory – the second is more difficult – an example described – the problem posed – reader's reaction to it – relevant questions before replying – why cannot the client decide? – the counsellor's description of the first interview – her query – her husband's behaviour – her parents – husband's hobby – the counsellor's reaction to her – his assessment and the prospect for the next interview – possible questions for the reader – comment on the counsellor's description – his attitude to the client – how would the client describe the first interview? – transcription of the second interview – comments on the client's difficulty – her marriage – her despair – positive feelings – evaluation of the interview – assessment of the interview by criteria listed in Chapter 6 – further aspects to be found in Appendix.

CHAPTER 10

Involvement

The purpose of this chapter is to clarify some of the factors that limit the usefulness of personal counselling, as outlined in previous chapters. There are people, circumstances and types of difficulty that help or hinder the process and therefore determine the degree to which it is helpful. The counsellor who expects too much will soon be disheartened, as will those who have not appreciated the constructive potentialities of a personal and therapeutic dialogue. The same is true of each client he meets. Either may expect too much or too little. And both are wise to pool their expectations and see what the one expects, demands or requires and what the other can offer.

The counsellor is responsible for assessing what may reasonably be expected from their work together. He can never be certain how much will be possible as this will depend partly on factors that cannot be seen at the outset. The first interview, however, can enable both of them to explore possibilities and decide whether to continue their work together.

Many counsellors are initially worried as to whether personal counselling may do harm, and it is usual to warn the beginner against involvement. These anxieties seem to arise from various sources. One is the unfamiliar nature of the work and the lack of precision in its terms of reference, the lack of a communicable technique in which he can put his confidence when he has to face the uncertainties of an unreserved discussion of emotionally-charged topics. He may then feel that his role is to be rigidly non-directive, always to keep cool and remote, objective and factual or deal only with externals and practical matters. But such a posture would defeat the purpose of personal counselling, however comfortable and safe it might be for the counsellor. What, then, are the risks of involvement?

In the most obvious sense, a counsellor might get carried away by his sympathy, protectiveness, partisanship or identification with his client and become involved in a relationship that is unconsciously collusive. This relationship cannot be constructive in helping the client to manage his own life more effectively. A counsellor may feel so sorry for a client (of either sex) that he forgets his role and slides unawares into trying to protect or comfort him, takes up cudgels for him, gives him money or forms a close personal relationship with him outside the counselling interviews. In such ways client and counsellor can get entangled in an emotional involvement with each other that springs from unconscious needs in both of them, for instance an infantile, defenceless dependence in the one and an inner compulsive need to be a benevolent protector, beneficiary, fairy-godfather or lover in the counsellor. It is a fine distinction between a caring, compassionate and constructive sympathy and this compulsive and unhelpful involvement. There are two useful safeguards (which any counsellor neglects to his own and his client's risk). One is to confine the relationship exclusively to the interviews. The other is to assess their relationship always in regard to the problems and difficulties in the client's life. Though genuine, sincere and truly personal, the relationship nevertheless exists within a professional context and for the purpose of enabling the client to manage his life more effectively. It is often necessary to remind a client of this as the relationship becomes more warmly personal, and sometimes it is necessary to remind counsellors of it too.

If we turn back to the interview we considered in the last chapter it is not difficult to imagine the counsellor feeling disheartened and frustrated by the negative quality of the client's attitude. He might also feel sorry for her and protective. She is greatly in need of help because she is unhappy, discouraged and hopeless. It is highly probable that she was not adequately cherished and valued early in life and so did not learn to be confident of her own worth. If she is attractive in perhaps a vulnerable, childlike way, the counsellor might want to comfort, cherish and encourage her rather than help her to face her handicap realistically and learn to deal with it. If he has a strong sense of chivalry or paternalism, if he is susceptible to the sometimes intense and defenceless charm that anyone of the other

sex (or sometimes a young person of the same sex) may easily
have for any counsellor, then he will become involved in the
unhelpful sense. Perhaps this would feel like benevolence but
in fact it would be a collusive involvement, inviting dependence
rather than self-assurance. On the other hand, he cannot help
her unless he is involved to the extent of recognizing her deep
emotional need. If he does not recognize this need, he may see
her simply as a woman with an impossible husband, or one who
cannot make her husband love her, or as a complaining woman
who is a bit depressed. His task, however, is not to comfort or
protect her but strengthen her to cope with her difficulty, her
handicap. He will therefore need to observe her reaction to himself and use it to enable her to see and face her incapacity.

In other words, it is no help just to warn him against involvement. He may, indeed, be too little involved in her predicament
to see what it is or help her to cope with it. If he remains totally
non-involved and non-directive he will deny her the opportunity
of recognizing her inner need and her difficulty in making a
personal relationship. Non-directiveness can be a useful part of
any interview from time to time, but it is always a denial of a
truly personal relationship. It is not involvement that is the
danger but being swept unawares into a role that is unhelpful
and will not enable her to cope with life more effectively and
rewardingly.

The harm that may arise from blind and collusive involvement is considerable if the counsellor is so undiscerning that he
is led away into a relationship that extends outside the interviews. This may injure the interests of them both, probably his
more than his client's. But such a development is so obviously
risky that he is, one hopes, unlikely to let it happen. He does
not need an attitude of defensive professionalism but a realistic
appraisal of her need and the way to help her.

If he does become collusively involved but manages to contain the relationship within the interviews, his client may at
first seem to respond well. That is, she will feel her personality,
her attractiveness are enhanced and she may be flattered and
pleased. This will be a useful stage provided the counsellor is
not led astray by it, for she may overtly or by implication try
to involve him more and more deeply. She would do this un-
knowingly, simply feeling that he was a marvellous counsellor,

a marvellous person and perhaps the first who had really 'understood' her. But sooner or later the counsellor will have to confront her with what is happening, and will have to resist her demands to make their relationship mutually dependent. Then she will feel hurt, angry and defeated. If the counsellor still keeps his head and sees what is happening, he can use this new phase to help her discover its resemblance to what is happening in her marriage. This is a delicate and skilled part of his work and if he can manage it sensitively it can greatly help her to face her real difficulty.

Involvement may also arise negatively, when a counsellor feels inwardly threatened or angry or anxious in his relationship. This, too, may arise with clients of either sex. The problem here is that he is likely to reject his client, either by not seeing his client's personal and emotional need and so concentrating on externals, or by being so unsympathetic, brusque or inattentive that the client does not return, or remaining distinctly uninvolved and non-directive in self-defence. No obvious harm arises from this negative involvement since the relationship is stifled and not allowed to develop. But unhappily it means that nothing useful has happened and the chance of helping the client has been missed. And it may be another experience of rejection for a client who already believes no one will accept him.

There is no simple device to avoid either of these hindrances to constructive work, so there can be no short cut. The counsellor's task is to recognize these involvements so far as he can, and then decide how to share them with his client as they arise. In the transcribed interview the counsellor had not begun yet to do this. But it was clear that he sensed what was happening by the explanations and clarifications that he offered to her. As she was still poised defensively between coming or not coming back, this was probably as far as he could go for she might easily have rejected him on the grounds that he was not helping her and had not enabled her to make up her mind. It is always wise to handle involvement delicately, offering a client an observation in the form of a tentative question: 'Perhaps that is how you see me, too? Do you think?' Such questions can be rejected if the client is not ready for the implications and the relationship will not be impaired. One can try again later when there is another example in what she is saying.

The question of involvement is central to the counselling relationship and is always a part of it if there is any effective relationship. The counsellor will be wise to do all he can to recognize in good time the effect that any client has on him. It is not always possible to do this for oneself, but in discussion with a colleague or a training group one can gradually develop this awareness. Better still, the counsellor who wants to fit himself as well as he can for this work might consider embarking on analytical therapy. In passing, I may be permitted to say that this suggestion is offered on the basis of observation of the work of other counsellors and on personal experience of counselling before, during and after some years of personal psychotherapy. It is incomparably the best form of training for work of the kind described in this book because it is the most effective way to come to terms with one's own unconscious involvement. It is, however, time-consuming, expensive and arduous.

It is sometimes said that counsellors may inadvertently try to solve their own problems through their work with clients. It is difficult to know what is meant by their own problems. It seems to me unlikely that involvement will lead anyone into identifying his problems with those of a client. It is much more likely that the client himself may present the counsellor with some kind of challenge that makes it difficult for the two of them to establish a free and open relationship. Each of them may project repressed aspects of themselves on to the other. It is an emotional challenge which, because of unconscious factors, the counsellor cannot fully recognize and therefore is not entirely free to deal with in the best way that will help his client. Short of analytical therapy, this limitation on his ability can be minimized only by case-discussion with colleagues or with someone more highly trained who is able to act as a tutor and, in a sense, counsel the counsellor.

Other limitations to the effectiveness of counselling arise from the client. His personality may be such that he is unable to enter into the type of dialogue we have been considering, even though the counsellor is fully able to accept him. This may be due to various factors. For instance, the client may be so emotionally shocked by what has happened to him that he cannot discuss it. He may be too distressed or too angry, too frightened or too anxious. This phase will sometimes pass quickly when it becomes clear that the counsellor does not put any pressure on him but allows him to take his time and express himself as best he can.

With some clients such receptivity and patience do not help and no significant dialogue can start. The counsellor may then have to postpone a discussion and do what he can to relieve the immediate situation. This may involve help of a different kind for the client, for instance seeing a probation officer or the police or his doctor. However necessary counselling may be in the long run, there may be more urgent matters to be dealt with before a start is possible.

This situation inevitably confronts the counsellor with the possibility that his client is psychologically ill. This is an area where he would perhaps welcome direct and unequivocal advice. Unfortunately it is as ill-defined as it is emotionally charged. It is easy to think that any client who cannot enter into an undemanding, patient, accepting and uncritical discussion of his difficulties must be emotionally sick. He may be. But the hold-up may be partially or wholly due to the counsellor's inability to understand him and enter into a dialogue in the client's idiom. There can be no easy or exact definition of emotional or psychological sickness and even psychiatrists differ among themselves. This makes nonsense of any attempt to draw a rigid distinction between counselling and psychotherapy, or between health and sickness, normality and abnormality. All too often such distinctions are arbitrary and based on a willingness or a refusal to regard the sufferer as a fellow being.

We may again consider the woman in the transcribed interview. Was she emotionally or psychologically sick or was she 'normally' distressed? Our answer will make a vital difference to the way we approach her. If we decide she is ill, we shall go no farther into her difficulties than trying to explain to her that she must be seen by a doctor or perhaps by a psychiatrist (if her doctor agrees). In other words, we shall tell her we cannot help her and counselling is no use to her.

But if we are not sure of this and try to understand what she is saying and how she behaves in the interview we may see that her predicament makes sense and that she is not totally shut off from discussion. Perhaps the idea of depression occurs to us, as it did to the counsellor the first time he saw her. She is gloomy and unconfident and she sees little hope that her predicament can be improved. This is characteristic of a depressed person. But does it mean she cannot be helped by counselling?

Some authorities would, I believe, say there is enough evidence to support at least the probability that she is suffering from some degree of depression. But what does this imply? Some would advocate no attempt at counselling with her until she has been to a doctor and been treated by him for her depressed condition. Others would suggest that, if her doctor will agree, she should be seen by a psychiatrist. Some non-medical counsellors have an unspecified faith in psychiatric treatment as a means of passing on a client they do not feel able to help. Sometimes they are wise to take this view. But sometimes they are running away from a situation they might otherwise be able to help.

There is a useful rule of thumb for a counsellor in this dilemma. If he cannot establish any productive relationship with his client, and if the client is as hopeless or depressed at the end of the interview as at the beginning, then without worrying about terminology or diagnosis it is reasonable to explain to the client that another kind of help may be necessary (at least initially) since their interview is not getting anywhere. However ill the client may be, this can be discussed with him and explained. Indeed it must be, because otherwise he will not agree to seek the medical help he may be needing. The decisive factor is not an accurate diagnosis or the accuracy of a technical term but whether or not a workable relationship can be established between these two people. If it cannot be, then other help should obviously be sought, with the possibility of counselling when the client is better.

In my experience counsellors are liable to underestimate rather than exaggerate the importance of depression. It should always be taken seriously because the possibility of suicide is never remote. Therefore if a depressed mood is marked and the client remains unresponsive, considering the kind of person he seems to be and the stress he is under, and particularly if he says that he gets such moods more or less regardless of circumstances and they alternate with feelings of happiness and optimism, it may be wise to suggest he tells his doctor how he feels and asks whether he can prescribe anything to help him. It is useless to try to cheer him up and risky to let him leave the interview as hopeless as he came in without having explained the wisdom of consulting his doctor. When he is feeling better, the counselling can usefully begin.

Another kind of person who cannot be helped by counselling is one who, in everyday language, has a tremendous chip on his shoulder and a rigid conviction that other people (or one other person) are trying injure him or get the better of him. This certainty may seem bizarre or absurd to the counsellor but he finds that it is quite impossible for the client to take any other view of events, or even consider that there may be another explanation of other people's behaviour. No, he knows they are against him and nothing will persuade him otherwise.

Such feelings are sometimes not amenable to discussion, or at any rate are unrelieved by discussion. Therefore counselling will be no help. All the counsellor can do is to try to help this person live his life more satisfactorily, on the assumption that his conviction of persecution (which may amount to a delusion) is true for him. These are very difficult people to help because they are unable to acknowledge any possibility that their conviction can conceivably be open to question. They are usually on the warpath and quickly abandon a counsellor as useless and try to take legal action or write to the Queen or the Lord Chancellor in a desperate bid to get their grievances righted or get protection from their enemies.

The counsellor need not fear that a friendly and accepting interview and an uncritical attempt to understand such a person can do any harm. But it is unlikely to be any help.

A useful guide for any counsellor is to see whether an interview of the kind we have discussed in earlier chapters seems to open up the possibility of a wider understanding of the difficulty facing the client. In spite of her hopelessness, the woman in the transcribed interview did respond and began to consider new possibilities. Counselling, therefore, was worth continuing, however slow any progress might be and however unrewarding it may be for the counsellor. The client came about her marriage and her husband's behaviour. But beneath both these is her own attitude to other people and her self-evaluation. This is not something that has arisen recently but, at least potentially, has been a difficulty for her throughout her life. She might have come to a school-counsellor or a student-counsellor with what would only superficially be another kind of problem or difficulty. Any counsellor may work mainly with people of a particular age group or in connection with marriage, delinquency or in any other context. The underlying factors are the same because the basic attitudes that affect our relationships spring from our earliest experiences.

A third group of limitations to the usefulness of counselling arise from the circumstances which limit discussion so that a useful, working involvement is ruled out. Our earlier consideration (in Chapter 2) of the practical requirements for this type of work illustrated the circumstances in which it is not possible to work in this way because of conditions, even when both counsellor and client are ready and able to make the attempt. However, conditions are seldom ideal and it is all too easy to blame them rather than recognize the subtler psychological and emotional factors that inhibit discussion and limit the establishment of an effective working relationship.

In a sense we have now come full circle and end as we began, with client, counsellor, and the difficulty that faces one of them. Counselling depends on the kind of relationship the two participants are able to establish. In social conditions of increasing depersonalization, the unique and creative capacity of individuals is consistently rendered subservient to technological, administrative and collective manipulation. The need for a fellow being with whom one can establish a truly personal approach to inner doubts, difficulties, anxieties and frustrations becomes correspondingly more urgent and more rewarding. Such an encounter can be, in the widest and essential sense, therapeutic. The quality of our relationships depends on the degree of integration we are able to achieve as individuals. And it is this cause that counselling can serve.

SUMMARY

Limitations on counselling – risks of involvement – unconscious collusion – counsellor's susceptibilities – his task – variations of response – rejecting a client – non-involvement as a defence – value of personal psychotherapy – projection – limitations arising from clients – psychological illness – depression – medical help – the test of a workable relationship – convictions of persecution – limitations from conditions of the interview – relationships dependent on personal integration.

APPENDIX

Analysis of the Interview

The short interview in Chapter 9 may be used as an exercise in perceptiveness and as an illustration of the processes of counselling outlined throughout this book. The counsellor, of course, had no time to stop and think. Neither did the client. But both of them had an advantage denied to the reader. They could see and hear each other and the more easily pick up some of the underlying feeling behind what was expressed. A study of the transcript does not permit this, but it does give one an opportunity to observe the unfolding of the interview.

The problem as originally stated was whether this woman should divorce her husband because he neglects her. But what is this in terms of the individual client and this particular counsellor? We know how he saw it, from his own description. What about her? She is unmistakably feeling rejected in her marriage. It has developed into a dilemma – either to put up with it or get out by breaking up the marriage. She cannot do either and so she seeks advice. She is not, apparently, a fighter though she did make her husband come home at least one evening a week. Otherwise she is hopeless and unable to do anything. Perhaps she has (as it were) retreated into despair.

Her opening remark (already mentioned in Chapter 9) contains both a threat (if he doesn't give her an answer she will break up the counselling) and also a subtle piece of cajolery (although he was no good, she has come back). This resembles the childish challenge 'I shall die and then you'll be sorry' modified into 'I nearly died and then you'd have been sorry' and also 'Look, I've come back, in spite of your being useless'. It is easier to recognize the threat than the flirtatious implication. 'I nearly didn't come back' implies an unsaid and arch 'But I did'.

Already one can see a link between her attitude to the counsellor and to her husband. Her husband doesn't *do* anything, he just talks (politics) and a similar criticism is by implication aimed at the counsellor. He only talked and didn't solve anything. This could be regarded as an unconscious sexual problem and it might easily have emerged as one. Quite possibly it would have done, had the counsellor been a woman. But the underlying conflict would have been the same, a woman feeling rejected, unloved, unwanted, unappreciated, unvalued. Such a situation has its roots in childhood, even in infancy, and in psychotherapy these roots would sooner or later be traced. If the counsellor is to help her, he needs to be aware of how fundamental such a conflict is and how hopeless it would be to try to solve it by good advice or by divorce or separation.

Her difficulty, however, is not only that she feels unwanted and rejected but that she does not know how to deal with this. She has not the ability to bring life into the relationship. Hence the curious shy remoteness and impersonality of saying 'one' instead of 'I' – 'what one does if one has to go on' (3) hence also the counsellor's dejected feeling after the first interview. She does not feel actively involved in the marriage, her only alternative to breaking it up is to go on and on, putting up with it. This theme constantly emerges in her remarks during the interview (at 3, 45, 47, 59, 61, 75, 89, 97, 117, 123).

But she cannot tolerate this prospect. And if counselling is to help her, it will have to be concerned with change. Sympathy is not enough if she is to be helped. However hopeless she is (and possibly the counsellor too), change is what both of them are looking for. Consequently we find the word 'change' (or 'changed') occurs frequently – twenty-one times. The theme occurs much more frequently than this, sometimes hopelessly, sometimes relating to the past, sometimes to possibilities. It will be seen in 23, 27, 33, 45, 60 and 61, between 65 and 71, between 95 and 108, at 119, 128, between 138 and 149, at 164 and finally between 177 and 191.

The frequency with which these two horns of her dilemma appear, in various contexts, shows that the interview is groping towards the fundamental difficulty. Indeed, there are only two passages in it where this dilemma is altogether missing. The first is sorting out her initial challenge (between 6 and 19), the other where the counsellor goes up a blind alley in exploring their reaction to having children and how it affected the relationship (the somewhat dead passage between 150 and 162). It was started by his sudden switch to a new topic. Such an abrupt change usually kills the dialogue for the time being though it is sometimes necessary if a counsellor feels an important possibility may be missed.

Perhaps the main theme of the interview is her inability to recognize that she can (or might possibly) play some part in improving the relationship. This is not a wilful hopelessness. It is much more fundamental and may be to some extent the cause of what she complains about. The counsellor realized this from the outset and described it at the end of his remarks before this second interview began. He brings it out into the open (for instance at 38, 48, 60, 98, 112, 134, 182), and this gives her a chance to see that the relationship has not always been dead. Early in the interview she says it has always been the same (65) but later she explains that it has not, that she used to go out to the pub with him, they did things together and were companions (119, 139, 141, 164–75).

This woman is specially vulnerable to rejection. Everybody is, though not to the same degree nor in quite the same way. To be rejected by the person on whom one is most dependent can be a shattering experience. It calls forth from some personalities an uncontrolled or even uncontrollable aggressiveness (in acts of reckless violence or compulsive infidelity, for example). In others the response is a retreat, a withdrawal that may develop into despair, depression or even suicide. Unfortunately in daily life such reactions often get little sympathy and are sometimes regarded as childish or infantile, in a derogatory sense. The roots almost always stem from infancy, since some degree of rejection by the person on whom one is totally dependent is a universal experience. Normally, however, such infantile experiences are not too frequent or too sustained and a child learns that he is valued and loved even by the one who must sometimes give her attention to others and cannot be present all the time. Others are less fortunate and suffer degrees of rejection that are more than they can assimilate. Then they are likely to remain specially vulnerable to situations that echo or reactivate these early rejection-experiences. The more severe these were, the less amenable they remain to conscious memory in later life. Nevertheless, a counsellor who appreciates their significance and is perceptive enough to recognize his client's reactions will be able to help her to cope with her difficulty better than before, partly through helping to clarify her handicap and partly by allowing her to form a reliable and realistic relationship with him during the interviews.

A second aspect of this wife's difficulty may also have unconscious roots. This is the response she makes to the threatening experience of rejection by her husband. Again, the counsellor can help her with this, even though his job does not involve bringing into consciousness the deeper roots of her reaction.

What does she expect of men? A proper man must do things, not just talk. He has all the advantages. Marriage for him is a convenience, somewhere to get food and be comfortable. The home is all his, he can go out when he likes and leaves no scope to fuss around him. There's nothing a wife can do about it. She cannot like it or like him by taking thought. She cannot change anything, least of all herself. She is left with two impossible alternatives, to put up with it or to break the relationship by getting out of it.

Such a person may be susceptible to any man who is active and dynamic enough to make a contrast to her husband (who may, in his turn, be discouraged by the feeling that he does not matter to her). If she is sexually attractive enough and not feeling too defeated or depressed, she may (as it were by accident) express at once her deep-lying aggressiveness against her husband and her infantile need for someone who will make all the decisions, and make it all come right by carrying her off. And then she will be swept off her feet by a love-affair until she finds once more that her basic demand of men is an unrealizable foundation for a lasting and rewarding relationship.

Beneath these reactions lies a factor that seems to play no part in the interview, namely the rival that her husband values more than he values her. It is only a shadowy feature so far, the pub. And politics. At a truly infantile level, total rejection means death. Too great a degree of rejection (although not total) leads to another kind of death, psychological and emotional rather than literal – a basic despair, a fundamental conviction that one is worthless, that life can only go on and on and there is nothing one can do to improve it.

The secondary factor involved here is the awareness that rejection implies a rival. One is left because someone else matters more. Later still these factors begin to polarize into the primary triangle of three people and two sexes. In these misty nuances of unconscious feeling lie attitudes that can be roughly paralleled by such expressions as these : the male is the all-powerful, privileged being, he can and should make everything all right, but he doesn't, he won't, he doesn't care enough, he gets elsewhere the comfort that he should be giving me, this is because I am useless and valueless, so there is nothing I can do, I can only put up with it, or finish it, nothing can change through me, only through him, and he won't do it.

This despondent and unfortunate woman is at present quite unable to recognize her own participation in the relationship, or even the possibility that she can participate in any significant way. This presents the counsellor with his own challenge, to enable her to discover something of her own basic attitude and at the same time to provide for her a chance to try out afresh a relationship that is uncritical, limited to the counselling, but within those limits truly personal. She brings her fundamental attitudes into the counselling and it will be within the interviews that she will have a chance to find her value and to reconsider her assumptions about men and the unrealistic demands she makes of them.

Finally, we should glance at some features of the interview which are significant for the task facing both participants. The counsellor's response to her initial challenge showed his willingness and ability to recognize and share with her (6) the fact that, as she saw it, he had failed her. Then he faced with her the basic stumbling-block to any possibility of progress, her feeling of hopelessness (48). He accepts this without trying to argue her out of it and without strongly reacting to the implications for himself, that she renders him symbolically impotent. She adroitly counters his attempt to get her to see her own participation 'You don't think there is anything you can do to change it?' he asks and she replies 'No, he'll never change' (60, 61). He refers to her relationship to her husband now and in the past, suggesting it does not seem 'awfully close'. She does not know how to reply. There is a pause and then she says 'I don't know, I suppose . . . yes, yes, I think so' (67). This theme is developed in what is, perhaps, the most significant part of the interview, where she starts by throwing the counsellor back into the role of adviser ('One just goes on. Does one?') and they consider the feelings involved in the relationship (89–137). The counsellor then summarizes the situation as he sees it, after perhaps rather aggressively facing her with her own inability to give her husband anything except food. Later he again summarizes the position they have reached, as he sees it (182), and this time she responds co-operatively, almost eagerly (183).

The interview ends with the equivalent of its opening. She, in effect, nearly doesn't come back. She repeats her challenge that if he cannot make it all come right he should at least tell her what to do (191), that she is quite capable of *thinking* by herself, if that is all that he can offer. He responds, in a sense, to the initial cajolery or flirtatiousness of her opening remarks by inviting her to come back and share her thoughts with him. To find that she can symbolically seduce him thus far is unconscious proof that she is attractive, worth caring for. Even at a conscious level the implication is clear – she is worth troubling about, though her own terms are not necessarily acceptable to the counsellor. He is there to help her, not merely to comfort her by doing or being what she wants. He will co-operate but will not be manipulated into playing a role that would please or flatter her but would not help her to resolve her conflict. His role lies between reality and fantasy, not as a compromise but a connection or a bridge.

SUGGESTED FURTHER READING

Almost all the books listed below have their own bibliography. By this means further reading can be extended almost infinitely. The following titles may be regarded as basic.

Berg, Charles, *Deep Analysis* (Allen & Unwin, London, 1946).

Biestek, Felix P., *The Casework Relationship* (Allen & Unwin, London, 1961).

Blackham, H. J., *Six Existentialist Thinkers* (Routledge & Kegan Paul, London, 1961).

Bowlby, J., *Child Care and the Growth of Love* (Penguin Books, Harmondsworth, 1963).

Bronowski, J., *The Identity of Man* (Pelican Books, Harmondsworth, 1967).

Brown, J. A. C., *Freud and the Post-Freudians* (Penguin Books, Harmondsworth, 1961).

Davison, Evelyn H., *Social Casework* (Bailliere, Tindall & Cox, London, 1965).

De Schweinitz, E. and K., *Interviewing in the Social Services* (National Council of Social Service, London, 1962).

English, O. Spurgeon and Pearson, Gerald H. J., *Emotional Problems of Living* (Allen & Unwin, London, 1965).

Ferard, M. and Hunnybun, N. K., *The Caseworker's Use of Relationship* (Tavistock Publications, London, 1962).

Fordham, Frieda, *An Introduction to Jung's Psychology* (Penguin Books, Harmondsworth, 1959).

Freud, S. *An Outline of Psychoanalysis* (Hogarth Press, London, 1949). *Two Short Accounts of Psychoanalysis* (Pelican Books, Harmondsworth, 1962).

Garrett, Annette, *Interviewing* (Family Service Association of America, New York, 1960).

Halmos, Paul, *The Faith of the Counsellors* (Constable, London, 1965).

Hollitscher, Walter, *Sigmund Freud, an Introduction* (Kegan Paul, London, 1947).

M   177

178   FURTHER READING

Jung, C. G., *Psychological Reflections* (Routledge & Kegan Paul, London, 1953).
　The Development of Personality (Routledge & Kegan Paul, London, 1954).
Kahn, J. H., *Human Growth* (Pergamon Press, London, 1965).
Klein, Melanie and Riviere, Joan, *Love, Hate and Reparation* (Hogarth Press, London, 1953).
Koestler, Arthur, *The Act of Creation* (Hutchinson, London, 1964).
Lomas, Peter (ed.), *The Predicament of the Family* (Hogarth Press, London, 1967).
Macmurray, John, *Persons in Relation* (Faber & Faber, London, 1961).
Pollard, Beatrice E., *Social Casework for the State* (Pall Mall Press, London, 1962).
Ratcliffe, T. A., *The Development of Personality* (Allen & Unwin, London, 1968).
Ruddock, Ralph, *Roles and Relationships* (Routledge & Kegan Paul, London, 1969).
Rycroft, Charles (ed.), *Psychoanalysis Observed* (Constable, London, 1966).
Stafford-Clark, D., *Psychiatry Today* (Penguin Books, Harmondsworth, 1952).
　What Freud Really Said (Pelican Books, Harmondsworth, 1967).
Steinzor, Bernard, *The Healing Partnership* (Secker & Warburg, London, 1968).
Storr, Anthony, *The Integrity of the Personality* (Penguin Books, Harmondsworth, 1963).
Suttie, Ian, *The Origins of Love and Hate* (Kegan Paul, London, 1948).
Tillich, Paul, *The Courage to Be* (Collins, London, 1962).
Timms, N. *Social Casework, Principles and Practice* (Routledge & Kegan Paul, London, 1964).
Various authors, *Relationships in Casework* (Association of Psychiatric Social Workers, London, 1963).
Yellowlees, Henry, *To Define True Madness* (Pelican Books, Harmondsworth, 1953).
Younghusband, E. (ed.), *New Developments in Casework* (Allen & Unwin, London, 1968).

INDEX